Chasing Hope

A mother's story of loss, heartbreak,
and the miracle of hope.

A Memoir by
Amy Daws

Published by Stars Hollow Publishing
ISBN 13: 9780990325208
Editing: Heather Banta, www.linkedin.com/in/heatherbanta/
Cover Photograph: Copyright © 2014 by Megan Daws Photography
Author photograph: by Megan Daws Photography
Cover Design and Production: Copyright © 2014 by Amy Daws

Some names and identifying details have been changed to protect the privacy of individuals. The author has tried to recreate events, locales and conversations from her memory. In order to maintain anonymity, in some instances the author has changed the names of individuals and places. The author may have changed some identifying characteristics and details such as physical properties, occupations and places of residence. The author may have also combined some characters for the sake of moving the story along. This book is not intended as a substitute for the medical advice of physicians. The reader should regularly consult a physician in matters relating to his/her health and particularly with respect to any symptoms that may require diagnosis or medical attention. The author accepts no liability or responsibility for any loss or damage caused or thought to be caused by following the advice in this book.

This book contains a truthful account of miscarriages with emotional scenes and imagery and expressive language.

Occasionally throughout this book, you will see:

***

This indicates a change in scene.

Often times, to switch between different pregnancies.

CONTENTS

Amy Daws

For all of my angels who are represented in the name
Nevaeh Peace.
Mommy misses you always.
I'll see you someday.

Amy Daws

PROLOGUE:

They said a baby born after a miscarriage or loss was a Rainbow Baby. It was supposed to represent a big, bright light at the end of a dark and scary tunnel. The beauty after a storm. But what happened when I lost five potential babies? Five babies. One. Two. Three. Four. Five. Five sets of fingers and toes I would never get to munch on. Five fuzzy heads I would never press my lips against. Five tummies I would never buzz and five pairs of chubby legs I'd never tickle. *Five deaths.* Before my nightmare began five years ago, five wasn't a very significant number. But when it came to dead babies, five suddenly became *very* significant.

Amy Daws

"Every experience, no matter how bad it seems,
holds within it a blessing of some kind.
The goal is to find it."

-Buddha

1: CESAREAN

Tears immediately sprang to my eyes when the nurse turned to look at her computer screen while she spoke on the phone at her large desk. "Yes, hello, I'm calling to schedule a C-section for Amy Daws on the ninth of May at…what time did you want Amy, morning or afternoon?" The nurse swiveled back from her computer screen and looked at me expectantly.

We had just finished up with another ultrasound appointment and had been moved from the exam room to the nurse's personal office down the hall. It was a small room that contained a desk, a filing cabinet and two padded chairs. Her desk was immaculate, aside from the multiple framed photos of her children and family on every staggered surface she could find. The window opposite where we were seated overlooked the hospital parking lot.

I never even glanced at my husband to see what he preferred in regard to the time slot, I quickly blurted out, "Morning."

She pivoted back toward her computer with the black office phone clamped tightly between her ear and shoulder."Yes, morning, 9:00? Okay, yes May ninth only puts her at thirty-seven weeks and five days. We're doing it early because she has an abdominal cerclage. Thanks Angela. Bye."

As the nurse hung up the phone, she turned to look at me and finally registered the emotion on my face. I did all I could to hold back the tears, but my vision blurred as the tears reached their spilling point. Her eyebrows crinkled tightly together as she considered my expression.

"I'm sorry," I said as the tears escaped down my cheeks in unison. "This is just such a big step; I still can't believe we made it this far. This is a big deal!"

Her lips pursed together in a sympathetic smile. "Yes, it is sweetie. You just cry all you want. This is a *huge* deal for you." She wheeled herself over to me and put her hand on my knee in a soothing, motherly way. The warmth and affection was enough to cause my eyes to release yet another flood of tears. I hastily swiped both cheeks and smiled awkwardly at her. Kevin put his arm around me as I exhaled a deep sigh. I felt the weight of my belly resting upon my lap.

My belly was really rounded out at that point. At five foot eleven, it took a while for me to really start showing, but I'd been obviously pregnant for quite some time.

I went to the ultrasound clinic every two weeks. I would always look around to do a cursory inspection of the bellies in the waiting room. Every time I was there it seemed like absolutely everybody was further along in their pregnancies than I was. I so longed to be the woman waddling behind a nurse on her way to get weighed and measured. Then, at last, the day came. I was so proud to *finally* be the big kid on the block—and to have the stretch marks to prove it!

I felt frustrated with myself and shook my head. "Ugh, I suck. Don't worry, these are happy tears. I'll be fine," I said in response to the nurse's concerned expression. I plastered a strained smile on my face. Kevin gave my shoulder a reassuring squeeze as the nurse looked at me awkwardly, apparently bemused at my choice of words.

"Yes you will, sweetie. Are you going home for the day?"

"No, I have to go back to work," I said as I situated my purse back on my lap.

She looked surprised. "Oh wow, you're still working? It'd be nice if you could take some time off before the baby comes."

I hated those statements. I called them *assumption comments*. Every time someone made an *assumption comment* about my baby coming and being healthy, and—well, to put it frankly—alive, I cringed inside. I fought the urge to look up to the heavens and plead. *No God. She didn't mean it. We aren't assuming anything. Please don't think we are getting too cocky down here.*

The fact was, I had my hopes up and prayed to God for a healthy baby every day for five years. It never worked. If you looked at my story as a whole, and you weren't scared, then you weren't paying attention. Or it would mean you had balls of steel. Everything went wrong with pregnancy and me. I even reworked how I prayed to God, thinking maybe it was how I worded it that caused all my pregnancies to go horribly wrong.

Back in the days of blissful ignorance, my prayer was pretty straightforward. *God, please allow me to become a mother. I want a baby to love and to hold and to care for. I want to give Kevin a child and grow our family. Help me on this journey.*

That prayer changed. *God, please let this baby live. If that is not your will—please give me the strength to endure.*

I had to add a disclaimer to the end of my prayers. A disclaimer! That's how messed up in the head I was over all I'd been through. So when people continually fed me full of those *assumption comments*, I had to throw a wall up for protection.

"I can't take time off before the baby comes. I have to save up my vacation days. But it's okay. I'm taking it easy." I said as I rose up off my chair. "I mostly just sit at my desk." That was only half true.

Kevin and I made our way out of the nurse's office and thanked her profusely. I always liked Nurse Bonnie. She had short, spikey hair and a very kind and nurturing way about her. I liked trying to remember all the nurse's names and was casual and friendly with them, like I'd known them for years. It really helped improve the overall experience with them. It made me more than just a number. They listened to me more closely. They were inclined to take more seriously any symptoms or anxieties. If they didn't know me, they had more of a tendency to dismiss my fears rather than listen to them. This was especially true with the ultrasound technicians.

I always teased them and joked around or asked them questions about their own kids. I noticed the more they knew me on a personal level, the more likely I was to get better, more thoughtful ultrasound photos. The self-educated nerd in me always loved knowing every exact thing they were looking at. If they liked me, they wouldn't get so annoyed with my fifty questions during the scanning process.

As we walked down the hall toward the busy waiting area, I looked over at Kevin. He was flushed red, and he beamed from ear to ear. He was so happy. I couldn't help but beam right back at him. But I still felt sadness and apprehension pulling at my heart.

Today was a very big step for us. We'd scheduled our C-section. I'd been pregnant many times before but had never gotten anywhere *near* close enough to plan a delivery date. What a milestone! I wanted to bottle up the moment and keep it for my rainy days, which were plentiful during my pregnancies and throughout my life.

We checked out at the front desk and rode the elevator down to the first floor. The elevator opened up to a lavish lobby area with couches, a coffee stand and people who were coming and going. Kevin handed our valet card to an elderly man in a vest. We held hands in the foyer while we waited.

"How are you feeling?" Kevin asked as he rubbed my hand.

"Pretty pumped!" I said with an edge of suspense in my voice. "I just wish we could fast forward and have our baby already! Ugh, I'm only thirty-three weeks right now, but I know that's considered viability. If the baby were born right now, odds are high she would survive. But now it's like, I'm almost full-term. I just want to get her out quickly before something bad happens," I stated sadly as I chewed my lower lip.

"I know, babe. We'll get there," he said reassuringly.

Another *assumption comment*, I thought. Ugh. Why do I hate those comments so much? Because I'm just a big ball o' crazy, that's why. Kevin should have known better than to say stuff like that. He knew me, and he knew I had every reason to be as crazy as I wanted. When it came to pregnancy stuff, every time I thought I was safe and things would be okay, some living nightmare would occur and slap me in the face and whisper to me, *you are not okay, I was teasing, you will never be happy.*

I swallowed that fear deep down to the dark knot in my stomach that had been a constant fixture in my body. I smiled politely at my husband. He was ever the optimist, and I loved him for it, yet I hated him for it at the same time. It would be nice if I could have blamed crazy pregnancy hormones for those contradictory feelings, but that was just my dazzling personality.

My husband, Kevin, has always been one of the good ones with a heart of gold and a sweet, yet awkward way about him. Sometimes he was so concerned with being nice and kind to people, he overcompensated and got tongue-tied. It was really funny. His overt congeniality had a tendency to make me feel like a jerk in comparison. I always prided myself on being a realist; I hated being fake. If I didn't feel it, I wasn't going to say it. Kevin was genuinely concerned about people's feelings. He made a big deal out of apologizing for things he didn't need to apologize for. Although it was good he worried about hurting other people's feelings, sometimes that nice-guy thing was a bit hard for me to deal with. But to know him is to love him. He's always adapted well in any social setting and been able to make friends with anybody.

Our differences complimented each other throughout our relationship in a weird, functional way and our friends said there was a definite role reversal in our marriage. I had a more masculine energy and Kevin was more compassionate and sensitive—too sensitive a lot of times. He would make a big deal out of nothing and spur arguments unnecessarily. I sometimes wished that Kevin could have been like all the other husbands I saw who were laid back and just went with the flow. But if he had been like that, I probably wouldn't have fallen in love with him.

I, on the other hand, was sarcastic and fought dirty; I didn't care as much about hurt feelings. Whenever we would fight, he hated to go to bed mad, whereas I had no problem falling asleep with a bottle of rage in my belly.

I wasn't a complete jerk though. I did hate when people were mad at me. I just didn't overreact to the little issues. If someone was seriously upset with me, the issue consumed me until I knew it was all resolved.

Fighting with my husband was a different matter altogether. He had to love me regardless because we're married. He's stuck with me 'til death do us part. So when we battled each other, it tended to get ugly.

We made our way out of the large glass double doors as the valet driver pulled up in our navy blue Chrysler Pacifica. Kevin opened the passenger side door for me and I clambered inside and immediately adjusted the elastic band on my maternity pants. Ah, maternity pants. I loved them and I loathed them. At times, they were freedom in stretch cotton. Other times, they felt like a pair of control-top pantyhose. I wondered if it meant my belly was in a constant state of expansion and throughout the day my pants actually got tighter. *What a scary thought.*

As Kevin maneuvered the car through the parking lot, he reached over to grab my hand. His hands were always so warm, dry and soothing; a welcomed contrast to mine, which were constantly frozen cold or clammy. If my hands were sweaty, he would comment about how gross they were. We were *definitely* past the "polite" portion of our marriage, and I was okay with that. I was never one to be overly sweet and sentimental, so comfortable and honest was a good place for us.

"Did you text everyone?" Kevin asked me.

"Yep," I replied and looked out the window.

"Cool, I'll text my family after I drop you off at

work."

"Work," I groaned. "I really wish I didn't have to go back. It'd be so nice to just go home, lie on my left side, and guzzle water for four more weeks," I sighed and looked at Kevin with a pathetic expression on my face. The fact that I knew guzzling water while lying on my left side during pregnancy was supposed to increase blood flow to the uterus, seemed to validate the endless hours I had spent researching getting pregnant, staying pregnant, increasing my chance of pregnancy—you name it. If it involved baby-making, I was in the know. I knew going back to the office wasn't the best thing to do, but taking time off at my place of work wasn't easy.

It was a small company with only seventeen employees, so when one person was gone, it was hard on the others. My job wasn't one that just anyone could jump in and do at a moment's notice. I worked as a commercial producer at a local TV station. I wrote, shot, and edited TV ads along with two other commercial producers. Since there were only three of us in the production department, we were assigned separate clients and worked individually on our own projects. It was a very creative process, which was what added to the difficulty of someone filling in for me when I was gone.

Also, I was really trying to save all my paid time off for when the baby did come. I fully understood that saving my time off and planning for the future with my baby was thinking along the lines of a *dreaded assumption*, but I couldn't help it. I was thirty-three weeks pregnant. I had to be smart about it. My office didn't provide an official maternity leave package, so saving my very limited vacation and sick days was crucial.

Overall, my job really wasn't that hard. Most of the time, I sat at my desk, but there were occasions in which some physical labor was necessary, like when I had to shoot video for my commercials. The bigger my stomach got, the trickier it was to perform the physical demands of shooting. I just sucked it up as much as I could. I had chosen a profession that was mostly male-dominated and there was no way I would show weakness because I was a woman in a man's field.

My office was small and the environment was laid back. Everybody except the sales executives wore jeans and even hoodies sometimes. A lot of the employees came and went whenever they needed to, leaving early for their kids' sporting events or heading out for doctor's appointments. From an outside perspective, that probably sounded awesome, but it was hard at times to look for somebody to ask a work-related question and they weren't there.

However, for all intents and purposes, this relaxed environment made it easier for me to suffer in silence with all my pregnancy neurosis. I couldn't imagine how difficult it would have been to be at a job where they noticed and cared if I was gone. There's no way I could have run out for quick, last minute appointments and various personal checkups if I had been a grocery store clerk or something. As long as I got my work done and didn't lag behind, I was able to fly under the radar.

The outside of my office looked like a rectangular concrete bunker. Just four thick concrete slabs and a steel roof. Thankfully, I had a pretty private office space, but it was attached to the two other commercial producers, so that was challenging at times, especially since I didn't get along with one of them very well. Of course, this man's office was only ten feet away and adjoined by a simple glass sliding door that he just *loved* to leave wide open to help me better enjoy the aromas that emanated from his ten-by-ten foot room. The man made no effort to be discreet about his flatulence. It was horrifying when people walked into my office. They'd get a look on their faces as though they smelled something peculiar but didn't want to say it. I knew what they were thinking: *how the hell does this place smell like a barnyard?* I constantly rubbed on strong, fruity, flowery scented lotion in attempt to keep our conjoined spaces from knocking people out cold.

I could have easily forgiven his flatulence if not for the fact that we had major history of conflict. Kip was his name. Was it just me? Or did his name almost *announce* he was a jerk? Perhaps I was biased because of my negative history with him.

This was my first job after I'd graduated college. Kip

loved taking credit for the fact that he'd hired me. But the truth was, I'd gotten myself the job. It was my demo reel, skills, and personality that made them choose me, not this arrogant man who thought he knew everything. We'd gotten along great until I'd stopped listening to every single one of his opinions in regards to my TV commercials. I'd started to feel confident in my own creative decision-making and began doubting how much he actually knew. We'd progressed into some pretty heated arguments over workload too. I felt like I did twice as much work as he did. So once I'd started speaking up for myself, it was the beginning of the end.

The real severing of our professional relationship occurred after one of my miscarriages. My third miscarriage happened right before our company Christmas party, so I had to miss the party because I was still physically healing. The Monday after when I went back to work, I heard from multiple people in my office that Kip had been telling everybody about my pregnancy and multiple losses and that I should "know better by now." The majority of the people in my office didn't even know I was pregnant or that I had even *one* miscarriage! I immediately charged into his office and confronted him. He denied everything and belittled me for being hormonal and emotional. I was so angry with myself for crying in front of him, but I couldn't help it, I was postpartum and suffering a tremendous loss. I was outraged that he thought he had *any* right to comment on my decision to try and have a baby. To say that Kevin and

I should "know better" was completely unspeakable. He had no right. To have a baby and a family was my ultimate dream and I wasn't giving it up for a rude coworker! The only reason I told him I was pregnant in the first place was because I thought he might be more willing to help me out if I needed it. I was one hundred percent wrong. Even if I didn't have hard evidence of what he said, it was obvious he said something and that was more than he should have. After that, just the sound of his name made my skin crawl.

At seven months along, I did everything I could to not ask Kip for help. Doing physically laborious shoots alone was not ideal, but I managed. Usually I tried to persuade clients into commercial ideas that were graphical so I could make the entire commercial without leaving my editing desk.

Often times, if a shoot was involved, it required a lot of squatting, bending, and lifting heavy bags of equipment. I relied on the sales executive, who usually wore dresses and heels, to help me. I'd be damned if I would ask Kip for a thing!

In any part of my life, I hated asking anyone for help. I was almost six-foot-tall—and no skinny rail. I grew up as the-son-my-father-never-had. I was the girl who helped move heavy stuff in the barn and did the majority of the physically demanding chores. People expected me to do the things grown men would do. I just got used to that. Asking a little five-foot-five sales rep in stilettos and a

Mark Jacobs wrap dress to help me haul a tripod, lighting kits, XLR cables and microphone cases wasn't an easy thing for me to do. As a result of my hatred of asking for help, I would carefully pick up one piece of equipment and slowly make multiple trips.

As Kevin dropped me off in the back of my office, I kissed him chastely on the lips and begrudgingly got out. I told him I'd see him at home in a little bit. I waddled my way up the short steps and through the shipping and receiving door that was just down the hall from my office.

I was so lucky I had it easy when it came to going away for appointments. I could go in and out the back door, and if I wasn't at my desk, nobody said anything. For all they knew, I was at a meeting or a shoot. Nobody had to know that I ran home at 9:45 in the morning to use my own personal Doppler to hear the baby's heartbeat because I hadn't felt the baby move all morning.

A Doppler is not a typical thing for most pregnant women to have. It was normally only seen in doctor's offices and the nurses used it to check the baby's heart rate while they waited for the doctor.

We got the Doppler from one of my many online friends after our first miscarriage. I had developed a following on my fertility discussion boards because there were so many who were brokenhearted because of my first loss. When I announced online that I was pregnant again, a woman contacted me through my personal email and said she and her husband also had hard times with miscarriages. They felt lucky to have had their baby, and they wanted to pay it forward. She asked if she could mail me the $150 Doppler, free of charge. Her only request was that when our journey was complete, we pay it forward to another online friend going through a tough time. We used it all the time.

As I sat down at my editing bay and shook my mouse to wake up my huge Mac computer screen, my coworker, Becky, popped her head through my door.

"Hey, you're back! How'd it go?" she asked as she came into my office and settled herself on one of the two mismatched cast iron barstools that sat behind my desk.

"Good, we got our C-section scheduled for May ninth," I said excitedly as I turned my chair around to face her. My big, black, wheelie office chair definitely wasn't comfortable for me anymore. It looked good with its smooth leather, high back and arm rests, but I oftentimes had to stuff my coat behind me to add pressure on the small of my back to relieve the ache I felt almost daily.

She raised her eyebrows. "May ninth sounds really good."

"We opted for a Wednesday because I've heard the

good lactation consultants only work on weekdays, so I want to be sure to have good help while we're there," I stated flatly. Gosh, I *hated* admitting I had those dang assumptions.

Becky's pale blue eyes turned wide. "Whoa, that's really close! This has gone really fast, Amy."

Fast. Was she kidding me? I had spent months, days, hours, minutes, seconds and nanoseconds fretting over every single twinge I felt. It didn't feel fast to me, not at all. I knew she meant well, but I wanted to tell her to try and spend thirty-three weeks constantly waiting for the other shoe to drop and see if she thought the time passed fast.

Becky started to look through the calendar on her phone to calculate exactly how many days were left until May ninth. I smiled warmly at her. Becky is a good friend, a motherly figure of sorts as she was thirty years older than me, but looked great. She had dark brown hair cut into a cute cropped bob and wore fabulous red-framed glasses all the time. I always said they made her look creative and artsy.

Creative was a good adjective for her because she had a tendency to be a little kooky sometimes. Becky had an absolute heart of gold, but the minute things got a little stressful, she lost her common sense. I couldn't help but love her. She cared about everything I cared about and she'd been with me through all of my miscarriages and heartaches. She had seen me shed the most tears, aside from my husband. Since I worked with her five days a week, year round, Becky had become a constant fixture in my life. She was like family to me.

The best part of it all was that the minute I needed to leave the office because I *had a moment*, she was always right beside me. We didn't go anywhere glamorous or anything. A lot of times we just went across the street to McDonalds to get an ice cream cone. We sat in her car and talked about my deepest, darkest fears and insecurities. It was extremely therapeutic to get it all out.

I was surprised she actually came back to find me to hear how my appointment went. Usually she'd forget I had one and I'd end up having to track her down to tell her everything. Becky could be a bit scatter-brained at times. When she was busy with work, she really couldn't multitask or think of other things. In all fairness, I had a lot of appointments, so unless someone attended the appointments with me, it would have been difficult to remember them all.

Becky stretched back on the stool, which was usually designated for clients to screen their commercials or edit along with me if the situation warranted. It was a great location for her to sit and gab with me.

"This little miracle will be here before you know it. I can't wait to babysit!"

I'm smiled at her, "Let's get the baby here first, Beck."

"I know, I know, but my God Amy, your belly is really getting big. Isn't this starting to feel real by now? I mean, gosh, that thing is rock hard!"

As Becky moved her hand around my taut belly, I looked down in a surrendering type of way, "Yeah, I know you're right. It is getting close, but I just don't like to talk about it too much, okay?"

That was enough said. Becky gave me a curt nod and stood up to leave, "Let me know where you want to go for lunch tomorrow. My treat!"

After she exited my office, I updated my online friends about finally scheduling my first C-section. Some found it strange to have online friends, but I wasn't online chatting or killing time on Facebook; I was making connections with others like me on *tryingtoconceive.com*. I had developed the habit of doing this after every ultrasound appointment.

***

Amy Daws

2: WWW.TRYINGTOCONCEIVE.COM

> *-Kathy, online friend*
>
> *"Aimes" was Amy's online name. We had never met in person, as we bonded on a trying to conceive website, but I often thought of her and all she had faced. Though I wouldn't wish infertility on anyone, I'm so happy we connected through our pain. She was an inspiration. My first and lasting impression of Amy is that she was the strongest person I knew. Not many people could go through what she had and come out of it at all, let alone, shine light on everyone she meets.*

Getting pregnant started off as a difficult task for me and Kevin. It took two years and nine months to be exact. We were married in August of 2005, and it was about a year and a half before we decided to start trying. We always knew we wanted to have children—doesn't everybody? At least everybody in the Midwest it seemed. It was just a matter of when.

That was the irony. I had lived my whole life assuming I would have a baby. I had a master plan: Go to college, find a good job, marry a nice guy, buy a house, get a dog, and have children. Essentially, live our lives in suburban bliss. That was the dream of everyone I grew up around, so of course, it was my dream too. I actually really loved children. As I grew up, I babysat other people's kids but it never felt like a job to me. Whenever we were at family gatherings, and there was a baby around, I was desperate for my turn to hold it. At church as a child, I would stare longingly at random families sitting in front of us with a new little baby. I was disappointed if I didn't know the family well enough to ask if I could hold their kid. To think I lived the majority of my life believing I had a *choice* on having a baby was laughable. I had no clue what I would be in for.

Regardless, I knew I wanted to wait at least six months after starting a new job before we tried to conceive. I graduated college in May of 2006 and started my job at the TV station immediately thereafter. The six-month wait was just my own personal choice. I knew I would feel bad if I started a new job and a couple of months later I'd make my announcement: *I'm pregnant. I know I haven't been here for long, but I will need twelve weeks off for maternity leave.* No one would get excited about that, certainly not the boss. I'm sure they would have faked happiness, but inside they would have been annoyed because maternity leave would have forced more work on everyone else.

For over two years, I peed on countless pregnancy test strips. All BFNs, *Big Fat Negatives*. I should have bought stock in First Response Early Result pregnancy tests. I alone could have funded one employee's 401K for the rest of his or her life. I was consumed and quite simply, neurotic. I had a PhD from *The School of Google Medicine*. I had declared myself a self-proclaimed expert in all things pregnancy and infertility related.

First Response Early Results were my drug of choice because they were the most sensitive pregnancy tests on the market. They had recorded HCG levels as low as 12.5, which is barely after conception. Those tests fed my obsession to find out as soon as possible. It enabled us to test sooner, know sooner, cry sooner, *or* be totally blissed sooner.

To help increase our odds of achieving pregnancy, I slept with my legs elevated as my husband's sperm percolated in my vagina all night. It wasn't glamorous, and it wasn't fun, but we had the system down. We would do the deed missionary style because we felt that position gave us optimum penetration. He let his sailors fly, and I held my legs up like a loon. Kevin went into the bathroom and brought me clean toilet paper. I would fold it up neatly and tuck it between my legs while he handed me my underwear and sweat pants. No sexy lingerie for this mama wannabe.

I think Kevin and I had sex every single day for twenty days straight one time because I was convinced we had missed our window. We had worked at it for over two years and knew how to get in and get out so we could go to sleep. Most men would be thrilled to have all the *hot sex* we were having. But men who had dealt with infertility knew it was not hot-and-horny sex. It was baby sex; it was forced, and it sucked.

It was difficult to know who to turn to for support. I constantly sought answers and ideas. I was desperate to hear stories similar to my own to give me hope that my journey would end with a baby.

My questions did not have simple answers I could locate from my *real* friends. Infertility sucked to talk about. I couldn't help but feel like a failure. I had hoped to surprise my friends and family with a fun announcement someday, so if I had discussed it, that would have spoiled the fun potential moment.

When I was brave enough to discuss my hardships with people, I'd heard the same inane remarks:

Just relax and it will happen.

Everything happens for a reason.

If you stop thinking about it, you'll get pregnant.

Maybe you should get drunk; then I'm sure you will get pregnant.

Those remarks made me want to puke. What was my response supposed to be?

Oh my gosh, you're right! That's what I've been doing wrong. Why didn't I think to just relax and stop thinking about it?

You're a genius, a God, a legend! You should write a book. You could call it 'Dumb Fricken' Things People Say to Women Who Want to Have a Baby, But Can't.'

I also had insensitive jerks that thought my talking to them about my infertility struggles was the perfect time for them to brag about how easy it was for them to get pregnant:

"Oh God, we just looked at each other and got pregnant. Do you want my kids?

My family is extremely fertile—we don't have any trouble with trying to conceive.

You don't want kids anyway, they give you stretch marks and they are a pain in the ass.

I also had to hear all the stories about how Rhonda Jane down the street wasn't trying to get pregnant and *poof*, she had twins. Fifteen-year-old Betty Jo waddled around at nine months pregnant, happy as a clam.

The stories that hit closest to home involved my brother-in-law and sister-in-law getting pregnant while they lived in a two-story walk up apartment. It wasn't that I thought they shouldn't have a child while living in an apartment building. I was just frustrated because Kevin and I had done everything in our power to be completely ready to have a family. We bought a big family house in a nice neighborhood with a good elementary school. It even had a fenced-in backyard and a park just behind our house! We traded in our two-door car for a crossover vehicle with third row seating and high safety standards. We were ready! It didn't matter that Kevin's brother and wife had ended up buying a house just like ours before their baby came. I was jealous and angry and wanted to savor in the injustice of the situation.

I think I was envious of Kevin's brother and wife, too, because I wanted to give Kevin's parents their first grandchild. Kevin was the oldest of his four siblings and I wanted him to experience the joy of providing the first grandchild. I suppose it was unnecessary competitiveness, but hell, I wanted it!

I knew I needed to find someone who could help talk me through the battles of infertility. Someone who could actually relate to my senseless thoughts and feelings! Someone who was going through what I was going through. In a desperate attempt to find solace in people I didn't know and wouldn't have the opportunity to murder in their sleep, I typed into Google, the ominous words:

Trying to conceive.

Suddenly, a whole *world* I didn't know existed was opened up to me! I met women who had problems similar to my own. Best of all, since I only knew them online, there was a brilliant degree of separation that kept my personal life and me safe inside my own head. I could share my deepest and darkest fears. I could spill my insecurities and the nitty-gritty details of trying to get pregnant without being completely embarrassed because I would never meet them. It was all at my fingertips, and nobody knew who I was!

Eventually, I was consumed with research and discussions. Even at work I was logged on to medical sites, social sites—anything I could find pertaining to conceiving a baby. My favorite website was about as subtle as one could get.

www.tryingtoconceive.com

Could the site be any more obvious? I would have loved to speak to the Webmaster of the site and complain to them. *Really sir, does the top third of the entire webpage have to display, in font size Seventy-two:*

TRYING TO CONCEIVE

As if being infertile wasn't a big enough issue to deal with, I had to worry about coworkers walking behind me and catching me in the act of wasting company time. I mean, help me out here. Why couldn't the banner header have been something incognito?

HOW TO IMPROVE YOUR PRODUCTIVITY

And then in small, teeny tiny letters after that:

Between the sheets.

That's a site I wouldn't be embarrassed about getting caught on!

There were websites where professional reproductive endocrinologists had their own discussion forums and were available to answer questions. So I got second, third, and fourth opinions from medical professionals.

When I was lucky enough to find a message board or discussion forum, the women I met had the potential to become lifelong friends. I was lucky enough to continue an online friendship with the same group of struggling mommies-to-be on a website for four years and counting. We would all log on daily and update each other on our cycles and where we were at in fertility diagnostic testing. We would sprinkle each other with "baby dust". We genuinely wished the best for each other: A BFP, *Big Fat Positive pregnancy test*. It was incredible the amount of hope I generated from women I had never met.

As many of them became pregnant, it morphed into a pregnancy message board, rather than a place to share stories about trying to conceive. Despite my fear that I would be the only one not joining the Mommy Train, I was so happy for them when their time came because I was with them during their scary moments. Countless negative pregnancy tests, failed IVF cycles, miscarriages, premature babies—you name it. We experienced it all together. It was my own personal network of hope.

After about two agonizing years of negative pregnancy tests, numerous tearful calls to my best friend, and daily prayers asking God why it had to be me, my husband and I decided to seek the help of a reproductive specialist, also known as an RE. Hopefully this guy could help Kevin and I get our mojo back since what we were doing wasn't working. It was then that our journey began.

Thankfully, we didn't have to go through the extremes of in-vitro fertilization (IVF). The women that underwent extreme levels of hormone medication that IVF entails were saints in my book.

The RE first had us try some oral medication to see if it would help me ovulate. When that didn't work, we moved onto some hardcore injectable medications to help my eggs do what they were supposed to do. There were some medical risks associated with taking the medications, a big one being twins or high order multiple pregnancies. The injectables were the types of medication the 'Octo-Mom' would have taken. It was a hormone medication, so mood swings were also a major side effect. Since they were a self-administered medication, the nurse had to give me a tutorial on how to inject in the abdomen at home. The needles were very thin, so the pain was minimal, but it was an intense emotional feeling to know I had to put a needle into my body just for the *hope* of having a child.

Kevin had his sperm tested and had good numbers. In the world of infertility, we were one of the *lucky ones* that still got to go home and do it the old fashioned way. Honestly though, if the doctor would have asked us to go home and use a turkey baster, we would have. We were that desperate for this to work.

After I did six cycles of the same medicine and received BFNs on all the cycles, I was super scared. We were closing in on two and a half years of trying to get pregnant, and I'd never seen a glimmer of a positive pregnancy test. At this stage in the game, I was willing to have a miscarriage just to know getting pregnant was a possibility!

Through all my online research and networking with other doctors, I discovered that because I had slightly elevated follicle stimulating hormone levels, or FSH, I responded better to a pure FSH medicine. FSH is a hormone that stimulates ovarian follicle growth. Follicles are essentially the beginning little eggs a woman makes when she ovulates. Up until that point, I did what my reproductive endocrinologist recommended, a combo FSH and luteinizing hormone med. I remember a time when I had no clue what any of that crap meant; by this point, I thought I knew just as much as the doctors.

Since I had been researching so much and disagreed with my doctor's protocol, he allowed me to try a pure

FSH drug I requested, called Gonal F. We got pregnant on the first try. No joke. It was the most amazing day of my life! I'd finally gotten a positive test for the first time in almost three years of trying. I took the test on one of those super-duper-sensitive brands that allowed me to test a week before my period was due. I think *I* knew before Christ himself did!

***

Amy Daws

3: IT'S A GIRL!

Desiree, Amy's Childhood Best Friend

*When the news broke that Amy and Kevin were expecting a
little girl, I thought, "That little girl is so lucky. So blessed. That
little girl doesn't know it - yet - but she would have the most
amazing, incredible, and strong mommy. That little girl doesn't
know it - yet- but her mommy was the bravest person she would
ever know." After all the pain, suffering, and heartbreak, no one
deserved the soft sweetness of a little girl as much
as Amy and Kevin.
A little girl—How absolutely perfect!*

The day we found out this thirty-three-week pregnancy
was a girl, I was really surprised. I thought it was going to
be a boy for some reason. For starters, through
chromosomal testing, we knew the majority of the babies
I miscarried had been girls. Concurrently, I thought the
odds this time would be a boy. I was only fourteen weeks
pregnant when we found out.

As I said before, I went in pretty regularly for ultrasounds. Having recurrent pregnancy loss automatically labeled me as "high risk". I had to have increased monitoring and ultrasounds. We went weekly during the first trimester and every two weeks after that. I read online that good ultrasound technicians should be able to tell the sex of my baby within twelve to fourteen weeks if the baby is in the right position. Sure enough, our technician was able to see it.

**

"Hey, do you think you could tell us the sex of the baby if you can see it?" I asked the tech as she squirted gel onto the ultrasound probe.

My feet were up in the stirrups and I had already scrunched my butt down toward the end of the exam table as directed. With the early ultrasounds, they used a vaginal probe to see the baby. The tech looked at me with a sly, skeptical smile. "I can try, but it really depends on the baby's position this early on."

She inserted a probe that looked like a long, slim neck massager with a condom wrapped around it; it never felt pleasant. The gel they squirted on the tip was always cold. Then they'd push the probe in until they found the area where it would insert easily. Some of them would push it into the wrong area and venture into the butthole region. I would promptly screech at them that they were too far back, and they'd quickly readjust. Most of them knew what they were doing though.

As soon as the probe was in, I looked up at the thirty-six inch flat screen TV mounted on the wall in front of the exam table. The lights were dimmed and Kevin was seated beside me on the bench. My purse, pants and underwear were all in a wad on the floor next to him. I instantly saw the dark black gestational sac that contained the baby. As she moved the probe around, I was then able to make out the shape of the baby's head and body.

I swear I could have been an ultrasound tech at that point. The first time I went through it, I had no idea what they were looking at. I wouldn't have been able to tell the head from the butt. Typically, the ultrasound tech would point out what was what. *There's the baby's head, heart, hands, legs, etc.*

I no longer asked the questions I once had. I asked questions with medical jargon slipped in. *What's the crown to rump length? Is the baby measuring on due date target? Is the yolk sac still visible at this point? How are my fluid levels? What's my cervical length? Is it over five centimeters? Are there signs of funneling?* I had technicians and doctors ask me if I worked in the medical field. I always told them, "No, I'm just unfortunate enough to be considered high-risk. I've had more ultrasounds than the Duggar Mother of the *19 Kids and Counting* reality show. I know what I'm looking for now."

The first thing I looked hard for was a teeny tiny flutter that was positioned right by the baby's chest. The heartbeat was the most important thing. The human body had always amazed me. We breathe in and out and our hearts beat without instruction. Regardless I always said a little prayer on the exam table right before the technician came in. *Please God, let the baby be okay. Please let her be healthy and strong with a good heartbeat and good growth markers. Please let her stay inside me until she is healthy enough to come out.*

I couldn't see the flicker of the heartbeat, so instantly I felt my own heartbeat increase as my legs tensed in the stirrups. Nervous goose bumps trickled over my head and shoulders.

The ultrasound technician continued her normal measurements. She checked my ovaries for cysts and measured both ovaries and then my uterus. She didn't seem to have a care in the world as I was in the midst of a silent panic attack. I'm sure I looked like I was doing fine, just waiting patiently, but on the inside I was anxiously screaming. *This is it! This is the day I lose my baby. The sex of the baby doesn't matter anymore. There is no heartbeat. The doctor will come in and tell me my options. They'll most likely suggest a Dilation and Curettage, commonly known as a "D&C," which is where they put me under, go in and scrape out the dead baby. It's happened again! What do I have going on at work? Oh yeah, I was supposed to finish an ad for that car dealership. The other commercial guy will have to do that. Will he be able to find the files on my computer? I'll have to call him. Gosh, I hate calling him. I hate asking for help. This is my fourth miscarriage now, what will people say? How am I going to get through this again? This is the worst moment of my life…*

Just then, Kevin interrupted my thoughts. "Ma'am, is there a heartbeat? I always look for it first and usually see it, but I missed it this time."

Her brow furrowed, "Oh yes, I saw it drumming away earlier, but we can check it out now if you would like."

"YES," I blurted. The huge knot in my throat broke a bit.

In that moment, I remembered how incredible my husband could be. Sometimes I thought he didn't get it. I thought he didn't have the emotional capacity to worry about something that wasn't physically inside of him. It took me by surprise when he practically read my mind.

The tech went back to her carefree attitude as though she was pondering what to eat for dinner later. I thought to myself that she had no clue how fricken' nuts I was going in that moment. She zoomed in to the flickering heartbeat. *Thank God.* She lined up her cursor and suddenly the computer speakers blasted. KAKUM-KAKUM-KAKUM-KAKUM-KAKUM- KAKUM-KAKUM-KAKUM-KAKUM. It was the amazingly fast and beautiful heartbeat of our baby. Sweet relief rushed over me. I had heard people compare the heart rate sound of a baby in utero to galloping horses, but I had never related to that sound effect. I think the sound of a baby's heart rate is as unique and individual as they come. I had enough of those ultrasounds to know it sounded good. The tech stopped the recording, measured between two waveforms, and the number came in at 162 BPM. *Perfect.* A bit high, since they say anything from 120-160 is normal. But I knew that slight tachycardia, also described as a tachy heart rate, wasn't nearly as concerning as a lower heart rate, known as bradycardia.

It was time to measure the size. *Crown to rump length, coming right up!* The ultrasound technician took the cursor and pointed it to the very top of the baby's head and dragged the line down to the tail of the butt, not the legs. The computer spit out a number that said the baby measured in at fourteen weeks and six days. *I'm only fourteen weeks! The baby is measuring large! This is good news! I can breathe now. Good heart rate, great growth measurements,* I thought to myself and then wondered if we could possibly be lucky enough to know the sex of the baby.

"So are you guys sure you want to know what you're having?" the tech asked with a knowing smile on her face.

"Yes!" I said excitedly. "We can't even keep each other's Christmas gifts a secret until Christmas time. We give them to each other as soon as we buy them. There's no way we'd ever keep this a secret."

"Well, don't paint the room yet, but I'm pretty

certain you're having a little girl." She smiled at us triumphantly.

Excited anxiety washed through my belly. I was surprised when she said we were having a girl as I was certain it would be a boy. But of course I was happy. I had suffered through multiple miscarriages in a row and never got far enough along to find out the sex. *If I'm not happy, I'm a horrible, sick monster.* It was just strange because I had it in my head it would be a boy. *But a girl! All right! Here we go!*

I looked over to Kevin and his face was red, red, red, which wasn't that uncommon. His skin was light, just like his mother's. Whenever he got worked up he turned into an over-ripe tomato. He smiled and leaned over to kiss me on the lips. It was that tiny bit of affection that snapped me back to reality as I felt a tear slide down my temple and into my hair.

My mind chattered on. *A girl. A buddy. A best friend. I can do her hair and teach her how to do her makeup! I wonder what she'll look like.* Suddenly, I was choking back more tears because the panic set in again. *Now if I miscarry, I'll know it was a girl when it happens. By knowing it's a girl, it humanizes this pregnancy that much more. She's so tiny in there, so helpless, I can't lose her—it will be entirely my fault if I do. I don't want to be too happy because I'm afraid I'll jinx this. Gosh, why can't I just enjoy this moment?*

"What do you think, babe?" Kevin asked

interrupting my thoughts again.

"I'm happy, it's cool. I had it in my head it was going to be a boy. I thought I knew, but a girl is great." A strained smile spread across my face. "We just have to get her here safely now. We have a long way to go."

The tech concentrated hard on the screen and saved the measurements and images she was taking. *She knew.* She knew because all of my previous losses were right there on the computer. In fact, when I got dressed and sat on the exam table and waited for the tech to come back in the room, I looked over at the monitor and saw thumbnail files of all my previous babies. My own little photo cemetery saved on their computer. How thoughtful. *Maybe someday I'll tell a nurse about how easy it is to see those images and how hard that might be for other women with losses,* I thought. I could handle it, of course, but if there were a way to stash those photos deeper into the online file so I couldn't see them quite so easily, it sure would have been nice.

4: NURSERY TALK

Rhonda, Amy's Grandma

When Amy sent me a photo of a mobile hanging in a nursery and asked if I could make something like that, I knew she had a plan. Being Amy's Grandma, of course I said yes, even though I didn't have a clue how or where to start. She picked out the colors that coordinated in the room and I set forth with the help of Google and a lot of prayers, to crochet around Styrofoam balls of various sizes. When it was completed, Amy's Dad and Kevin hung them with fishing line over the crib. While I worked on the mobile, excitement and anticipation kept building about the arrival of a baby to occupy the nursery. I recall when Amy had her first miscarriage how bad Grandpa C felt when he first heard that news. Tears filled his eyes, as he did so love little babies. He said, "Oh, Kevin and Amy would be such good parents, but God must have a different plan for their lives." He'd passed away, but with God's help, we knew he was taking care of the little ones in Heaven. I felt honored to have had a part in sharing my talents for Amy and Kevin's upcoming miracle.

I got home from work around 5:30 PM. I pulled into the driveway and walked into the house. I heard Kevin pace up and down the hallway as he talked to his mom. He always paced when he was on the phone. It was so annoying. Whenever I watched something on TV, he would talk loudly on his phone and pace right into the living room, and I was unable to see or hear anything. *Great. Thanks, babe.*

Kevin raised his head, acknowledging my arrival. He was still beaming about scheduling our C-section that day. We really had come a long way from all the others.

I sat my big purse down on the counter, poured myself a glass of apple juice, and made my way over to the couch. The couch was my trusty steed. We had become very close during the pregnancy. A doctor had never put me on bed rest, but I was always achy and crampy, which the doctor continued to tell me was normal, so Kevin and I decided I just needed to take it easy whenever I was home. I was definitely cool with that.

I sipped my glass of apple juice while lying on my left side. I immediately felt the baby fluttering inside me. Although, they were definitely more than *flutters* at that point. At thirty-three weeks pregnant, baby movement was incredible. I couldn't begin to describe the amazingness of a baby moving in my body. It was so crazy to think about. I remember when I first felt the baby move. I denied it for a long time because admitting it would have felt like I was tempting fate. Admitting it would have felt too real. I was constantly trying to protect myself from getting too attached because I always assumed things would end badly.

The phone rang and I heaved myself up off the couch and dug it out of my large green Guess purse. As I saw *Home* come up on the caller ID, I knew it was my mother. My dad never called, unless he had a few rum and diet cokes and my mom left him home alone for the evening. I was twenty-eight years old and still had my parents' number set as *Home*. Kevin and I had been in our house for seven years and I *still* considered Mom and Dad's house *home*.

"Hello?" I said as I settled myself back on the couch.

"Heeey, how are ya?" my mother's voice pealed through the phone.

"I'm good. Hanging in there."

"That's awesome about your ultrasound. I got your text. Our little peanut is growing like a weed in there."

"Yeah, the nurse said she's already seven pounds. It's a good thing I'm a planned C-section because I just know I'm going to have a twelve pound baby."

My lips pursed together as I cringed at my words. Every so often, I slipped up and spoke just like everyone else. *Assumptions.* I would make a statement *assuming* my baby would be coming large, alive, and healthy. *Dammit. I should know better.* I knew when I said it and immediately regretted it.

"And your cervix looked long and closed, or whatever it is you tell me they like to see?"

"Yes Mom, it was long. Still over five centimeters and no signs of funneling or anything," I said as I shifted awkwardly on the couch with my glass of apple juice.

"Good, good. This is good! You're thirty-three weeks now. You just have another month, and this little miracle will be here for all of us to see," my mom said as she used her sweet voice.

My mom was a short, round woman with nearly white hair. At a very young age she would use boxes of hair color to hide the early graying. Eventually she must have given up because the majority of my memories of her included short, gray, *mom hair*. It suited her and it was an attractive gray. She was over fifty, and it was starting to turn white, just like my grandmother's. The two of them could have been twins.

My mom and I had a good relationship at that point. In my younger years, it was rocky. I was a bit of a wild child and my mother was a control freak. It was a lethal combination in the heat of a battle. As soon as my mother turned on the tears, the guilt that rippled through me was enough to make me sick. I hated to see my mother cry. I suppose most kids would.

My dad was short and round just like my mom. My height must have come from my Grandpa C, who had passed away just a few years prior. I was easily a whole head taller than both of my parents. My grandpa was a tall, slender farmer with dark, leathery skin from years of farming and raising animals. I loved my grandpa, and I still missed him all the time. It broke my heart to know he would never hold or meet my earth baby. I tried to comfort myself, knowing he was probably teasing all of my angel babies in heaven. I was glad they had him. He was funny in an odd sort of way, always making weird jokes that confused us, but loved making all seven of his granddaughters smile.

"Tell her she should take a couple of days off and relax before the baby comes," bellowed my dad from somewhere in my parents' house.

"Did you hear him?" my mom asked.

"Yes, I heard him. I'm not going to do that Mom. I don't have the extra vacation. I can sit at my desk as easily as I can sit on my ass at home. Pretty soon I'll tell everybody I just can't go on shoots anymore. One of the other production guys will just have to pick up the slack." I sighed at that annoying thought.

When my dad tried to get me to slow down or settle down, it always worried me that he too wasn't sure if the baby would make it. That freaked me out because I was a constant pessimist when it came to the pregnancy. If the world and the people around me started to believe me and agreed with all my crazy paranoid and cynical mumbo jumbo, where would that leave me?

"Well, you just take it easy as much as you can and walk slow wherever you go."

"Jeez Mom, you sound just like Grandma!"

My mom chuckled a little on the other end of the line. She didn't mind one bit being compared to her mother. She was used to it.

"Well, ol' Grandma might know a thing or two! I'm looking out for my future grandbaby in there."

Her reference of a grandbaby brought a little knot into my throat. I quickly swallowed it down. "Thanks Mom. I know. I'll be careful."

"And tell that good-for-nothing husband of yours to take good care of you," roared my father again. I could hear a smile behind his sarcastic tone.

"I will, Dad. Talk to you guys later," I said loudly to both of them. I hung up the phone with a smile.

My father loved my husband. They were two peas in a pod. Kevin was my dad's favorite drinking buddy. On weekends when we would travel the two hours home to visit them, Kevin never said no to a Bloody Mary at 9:00 AM on a Saturday morning. That was pretty cool, in my dad's book.

My dad always had a soft spot for me. I was his little

helper on our acreage, the son he never had. In High School I was heavy into sports, basketball especially. That was tough because I was never any good. But man did I try. In my teen years, we'd have late night conversations after a tough game where I didn't get much playtime. It broke my dad's heart as much as it broke mine. He always told me I had more heart than any of those other girls put together. "You try so hard, kid! You play great defense, and DEFENSE wins ball games. You deserve to be out there. That coach needs to take that stick out of his ass."

I knew part of him was right, but I also wasn't quick enough on the basketball court. I'd throw up at the first practice every year because I never pre-trained. But I loved the game. I loved being on a team and feeling the camaraderie with a bunch of girls I traveled with and communicated with on and off the court. But I still got chills down my spine when I heard the sound of basketball sneakers squeaking on a gym floor. Ugh, it makes my chest hurt just *thinking* about all the running we had to do!

I heard Kevin in the hallway as he wrapped up his phone call with his mom. He walked out taking his typical big, long strides. I always marveled at how tall and broad shouldered he was. He stood about six-foot-two and had dirty blonde hair that was thinning a bit on the top, no thanks to the years of life we'd probably lost living through so many of our worst nightmares. He had just gotten a haircut, which is when he looked the sexiest.

Something about that perfect shaved hairline right at the nape of his neck, made him look good.

"Hey Babe, how you doing?"

As I let out a relaxed sigh, I said, "Good. Talking to your mom?"

"Yep," he said as he sat down in our big brown, overstuffed armchair.

"Telling her about the baby?"

"Yep. She's excited for us, I can tell. She asked if you were really starting to show a lot and I said you have been for a while. Although I've noticed more today than I have this whole time."

"Really? I wonder why. Do you think the baby shifted in there or something?"

"I don't know," he said as he scratched the top of his head. I always winced a little inside when he did that because I felt like he was scratching his hair permanently off! "You feeling okay?"

"Yeah, just crampy as usual. If we hadn't just had an ultrasound today, I'd be using the Doppler, that's for sure."

"You feeling her move a lot?"

"Oh yeah, she's moving right now. It's funny though,

she can be wiggling and moving like crazy and while that does make me feel less worried, I can still get myself in a tizzy thinking maybe she's going down into the birth canal. Or maybe she's moving because the cord is wrapped around her neck. I'm one f'd up lady."

"I know it's hard, babe, but we'll get there. We need to start getting excited. Actually, we probably should start working on the baby room!"

Immediately I got a sick feeling in my throat, like my tonsils were trying to crawl out on their very own. The baby room was a constant anxiety for me. Anxiety because I knew it needed to get done. And anxiety because what if we got it done, and it was perfect and everything I imagined it would be, and no baby came home to it? How could I handle that? How could I face a beautifully decorated nursery if I lost the baby? The thought was enough to make my stomach roll.

I heaved a big sigh and sank back onto the couch. "I know, you're probably right. I've been looking at ideas online, so I'll get talking to my mom and grandma. There are some things I'm hoping they'll make for her room."

Kevin made his way into the kitchen, most likely to try and figure out what we could eat for dinner. "Well, you better talk fast because if it's stuff that will take them a lot of time, they don't have much of it left."

I knew he was right. I already had a small collection

of baby things that had accumulated from friends and family as it was. The first time I got pregnant, my friend Ashley gave me two baby outfits right away. She was so happy for me because she knew it took us so long to conceive in the first place. One was an adorably pink, girlie fleece number. The other outfit was more unisex, with yellow ducks. They hung ominously in the room we planned to use as the nursery.

Earlier that year, at Christmas, my two sisters surprised me with gifts for the baby. I was about seventeen weeks along, which was a huge feat in itself, considering my history. My parents, sisters, their husbands and Kevin and I all sat around the great room at my parents' big cabin-style house on a lake. We all noisily opened presents one at a time. My nephews were bursting with all the Christmas excitement. I was a bit confused because I had an extra gift and my mom was always very mindful about making sure everyone had an equal number of gifts to open on Christmas.

I glanced inside the gift bag and saw light, baby-pink. A huge wave of emotion rolled over me and realization set in: this was a gift for the baby inside my tummy. I felt tears in the back of my throat. With that, I instantly sobbed and my eyes welled up within seconds. I tried to awkwardly laugh it off, but it was no use. Both my sisters and my mom looked over at me with pained smiles while unshed tears welled in their eyes.

I carefully opened the gift bag to reveal a couple of

simple baby rattles, a package of pink baby onesies, and some bibs. It was a Christmas gift for my baby. This was a first. I was overwhelmed at the acknowledgement that this baby was different from all of the others. Giving me this gift showed me that they, too, had *hope*.

***

Amy Daws

5: FACEBOOK OFFICIAL

Becky, Amy's Coworker & Friend

Amy and I shared a special bond. She was my co-worker and friend, but being the same age as one of my own daughters, I couldn't help but look at her in a motherly way. Because of that closeness, just like I had with my two "real" daughters, when she hurt, I hurt. I watched her highs and lows with each pregnancy. Highs with the initial news she saw a positive on the pregnancy test, and the scary lows when things went wrong. I so wanted to put my arms around her (which I did do!) and take away all her pain and suffering. But I couldn't, and I felt helpless. My heart broke each and every time she told me the terrible news of her miscarriages. I heard those sad words too many times. It just wasn't fair. Amy and Kevin deserved to have a child more than anyone, and it just wouldn't happen. I knew she needed to find someone who could really give her the help she needed.

The first time I ever got pregnant was unforgettable. I called the clinic and told them I had a positive test at home, so they had me come in for blood work. They called me a few hours later to confirm that I was indeed pregnant. I left my office immediately and drove straight to Kevin's office. I called him and said, "Come outside. Hurry!"

He came out of the door with a knowing expression on his face, and I ran into his arms and exclaimed, "It's real, babe. We're really pregnant!"

He hugged me hard, and his eyes misted over. It was an amazing day.

It was an amazing pregnancy. I had some spotting and bleeding issues here and there, but my reproductive endocrinologist said that was normal for some women. He said it was no big deal as long as the baby grew and had a good heart rate. He saw us every week as our little bean slowly transformed into a little baby. Weeks six, seven, eight, nine, ten—all perfect ultrasounds. I had a stack of flawless take-home pictures. Already, our little bean had enough pictures to fill an entire photo album.

After a great eleven-week ultrasound, the RE said he was going to release us to an OB/GYN because everything looked good and this was as far as he could take me. We planned to see her at the twelve-week mark. Since I'd still been spotting, she said she'd do another ultrasound. Amazingly, the baby wiggled around on screen. That was a first for us. I couldn't believe it. It almost looked like it was flinching and flexing or something. It was amazing. The OB/GYN congratulated us and said she was so happy for us after all of the time it took us to get there.

I went back to work after our appointment and started cramping a lot. I called the nurse, and she said the cramps were very normal after doing the routine pap smear that day and that it was nothing to worry about. She suggested I go home, take some Tylenol, and just take it easy.

I went home and relaxed. My bleeding gradually increased throughout the night. Then at around 10:00 PM, I reached my breaking point.

After I rolled around uncomfortably in our bed, I finally shook Kevin awake. "Babe, these cramps are so bad I can't even sleep. That's not good, right?"

"What do you want to do? You want to go to the emergency room?" he asked sleepily.

"I think we have to. This can't be right," I said as the anxiety built inside me.

At the ER, we sat in the waiting room anxiously and waited for a nurse to call us back. I wanted to use the bathroom because I could tell the bleeding was very heavy, but the receptionist told us I couldn't in case they needed a urine sample. After waiting for fifteen minutes, we finally got into an exam room. The doctor came in shortly after and informed us that he was first going to do a pelvic exam to see what was going on and then would decide if we needed another ultrasound.

While my legs were in the stirrups, he used silver, sterile forceps and repeatedly pulled out clots of blood and tissue. He then handed them to a nurse who stood there with a pink receptacle.

I lay on my back looking up into the florescent lights, just bawling at the disgusting inhumanity of the situation. Kevin rubbed my arm affectionately while he watched what the doctor was doing. I wasn't sure what the heck was going on with me, but I knew it couldn't be good.

The doctor gently tapped my leg. "Okay, you can sit up now."

I did so, awkwardly, and noted a grave look in his eye. "I'm sorry to tell you, but I just pulled the baby out."

It was like the wind had been knocked out of me.

"The baby was lodged in your vaginal walls. There was no way to save it," he said sympathetically.

I stared at him, horrified, my eyes still wet with tears. Kevin looked at the doctor, shocked and scared. Heartbreak eventually smeared across his face.

I knew something bad was happening, but for whatever reason, my mind didn't know what the doctor was going to tell me. What the hell was wrong with my brain that caused me to think the baby might still be alive after he had continually pulled bloody goo from my vagina for ten minutes?

I urgently replied, "But we just had an ultrasound today, and everything was fine!" My mind reeled as I thought to myself that this couldn't be happening.

The doctor gave me some song and dance about it being God's plan. He then suggested perhaps the baby wasn't healthy, and that's why it happened.

I slowly tuned him out as I grew increasingly frustrated. How did God's plan include getting us all the way to twelve weeks, *the supposed safe zone,* only to rip the baby away from us? How did God's plan involve us having weekly ultrasounds that led up to that moment showing nothing but a perfect baby? If it was true, then *God's plan sucked.*

"You can see the baby if you'd like, but I don't recommend it. It's really not going to be what you expect," he stated simply.

Kevin just looked to me and waited for an answer. I silently shook my head no. "That won't be necessary. But I would like to request fetal testing on the baby to check for abnormalities or something."

The doctor looked at me thoughtfully. "We don't typically do fetal testing on first losses, but since you are twelve weeks along, this is technically a second trimester loss, so it would be appropriate. I'm still going to order an ultrasound to check for any retained tissue."

I recoiled. *Retained tissue? Like, chunks of my baby? Oh my God. This is a nightmare.*

The ultrasound technician came in the room and began setting up for the exam. She looked sad and thoughtful. As she inserted the probe in my vagina, I could see the images on the monitor. If the loss of our baby hadn't fully set in yet, it did in that moment. On the screen, all I could see was black nothingness inside my uterus. For twelve weeks, we had six perfect ultrasounds and a perfect gestational sac with a growing baby inside. We saw that baby every single week, growing and moving inside me. I had become accustomed to seeing it in there. Now it was just an empty uterus again, like it had been for so long before.

When the tech left us, the severity of the situation had finally set in. I was angry. I was *really* angry! I sobbed and screamed out at Kevin, "This is just fucked up! How did this happen?"

I threw my legs off the side of the bed, and I ripped my IV out of my hand. I was briefly thankful for the searing pain because it gave my heart a small break. I squeezed my hand where it ached, holding the blood in with pressure and sobbed violently.

Kevin rushed toward me with his arms outstretched.

"Stop, Amy, stop!" He clamped his arms around over the top of mine and begged me to calm down, tears streaming down his face. He hurt just as much as I did, but I couldn't stop.

I screamed at him, "WHY THE HELL AREN'T YOU PISSED? We are so screwed, Kevin! This is it. It took us three years to get here. Three fricken' years! It's all over. It's over. We are fucked! We're so fucked."

I collapsed on the bed and bawled as I struggled to catch my breath. It reminded me of a cry that I'd only ever done as a child, gasping as I felt the heart-wrenching pain in my chest. My throat ached, my face burned, and my chest felt like it was going to explode. There was nothing in me anymore. Nothing. I was a shell of nothingness.

Kevin held me tightly until the nurses came back with our discharge instructions. It was nearly 2:00 AM before we left the emergency room. I was in a lot of pain and still cramping and bleeding. The doctor gave me a prescription for pain pills that we were to go and fill at a twenty-four-hour pharmacy.

Kevin drove silently, and we both just stared out the car windows, numb and in shock as tears spilled freely down my cheeks. The stoplights flashed yellow because of the late hour. When Kevin parked, a single security light illuminated the inside of the car.

"Hey, I'll go in and get the prescription. You just wait in the car. I'll need your insurance card though," he said quietly.

I reached inside my purse for my wallet, and he quickly grabbed my bag out of my hands, rummaging awkwardly. As he opened my wallet, he turned away from me.

Curious, I leaned forward and looked over his shoulder. It was then I saw him fumbling hurriedly with all our ultrasound pictures that I had kept in my wallet for weeks. Frantically he attempted to stash them away and out of my line of sight. I looked forward and shook my head.

My husband tried to spare me the pain of seeing our baby who was no longer inside me. When he realized he wasn't as subtle as he'd hoped, he looked at me apologetically and rubbed his hand on my arm.

"Just go," I stated coolly, my face sneered with disgust.

He set the pictures on the dash of the car and walked into the pharmacy, shoulders hunched.

I hesitantly grabbed the photos and flipped through them; tears streamed down my face and fell directly onto the images. Our baby went from a tiny circle of digital goo, to a tiny bean, to a tiny tadpole, to a tiny baby. There was a picture of the baby's hand in a waving motion, like it could have been saying, *Hi Mom. It's me. Don't worry, I'm worth it.*

We got home and crawled into bed to hopefully sleep away the pain. We both took three days off of work that thankfully led us into the weekend so we had five full days to mourn the loss of our first pregnancy.

Not only were we mourning the loss of our baby, we were mourning the loss of our *hope*. It took us nearly three years to achieve this pregnancy. It had been three long years of unfulfilled dreams and countless negative pregnancy tests. I was despondent. How could I not be?

My mother came to visit and be there for us any way she could. She made cheesy potato soup, which would forever be a memory of my miscarriage. It was creamy, warm, and soothing. Sadly, that soup would be made many more times to help comfort us in our time of need.

In those days of remorse, I discovered how amazing sleep was because it allowed me to forget the pain for the few hours I remained asleep. Waking up was the hardest thing. Each time I woke I had to deal with the pain all over again. As soon as I opened my eyes, my memories rushed back into consciousness, and the sobs would hit. Kevin would wake to my cries, and all he could do was hold me. He would hold as tightly as I could take, until the memories fully sunk in yet again.

On top of it all, I had to tell our friends and family

about the loss. When I was eleven weeks pregnant, I was stupid enough to post our long-awaited news on Facebook, so *the whole world* knew. I thought I was doing pretty good waiting until eleven-weeks along. I'd seen others post their news the same day they peed on the damn stick.

I received so many well-wishes and congratulations and now I had to go online and say: *Just kidding everyone. We are no longer pregnant. Our baby is dead now. LOL.* But it was no laughing matter.

Having told a group of people I was pregnant and then having to tell them I lost the baby was about as fun as I would imagine it would be to trip and fall on my way onto a stage to accept an award, only to get up there and have them say, *'No, not you, the other Amy.'*

The worst part was I couldn't say how I really felt because the general public wouldn't be able to handle the truth. Had I been able to say what I truly felt, it would have come out a whole lot different.

We lost our baby and feel like shit. We feel like God took a big dump on our hearts, and slapped us in the face. Not only did we lose our baby, we lost our baby in the supposed safe zone. Twelve weeks is supposed to be the time when my risk of miscarriage went way down. Snap. Guess the joke's on us! And bonus: it took us three years to get pregnant in the first place, so now we're really fucked. We feel miserable and can't talk about it without crying, so please don't say anything to us about it.

Instead, I wrote this:

Kevin and I suffered a miscarriage at twelve weeks pregnant. It all happened suddenly and was a huge shock to all of us, including our doctor. We hope that everyone will keep us in their thoughts and prayers. I know that one day, we will find a way to accept this and move on—but for now, it just sucks.

About a week after the loss at a follow up appointment, I was told that not all the products of conception had bled out. I'd have to have a D&C. They would have to go in and scrape out the remaining bits of the pregnancy. I felt numb when they told me the news. It was the equivalent to kicking a man while he's down. I just desperately wanted this nightmare to end. Kevin was out of town for work and it tore him apart that he wasn't able to be there for me. My older sister, Amber, came with me and helped me through the anxiety. She had the genius idea of telling the anesthesiologist that I get extremely anxious during procedures and surgery and wondered if there were any drugs that could help calm my nerves. Boy I was glad she was there. But nothing could numb the pain I felt waking up in post op'. I was crying so hysterically, the nurses had to bring my sister back to help calm me down. I'd never forget the empty feeling inside me. Every bit of my baby had been scraped out until there was nothing left.

About three weeks after the D&C, we got the genetic testing back regarding the baby. I was at work when the call came from the nurse. I took the call in the studio attached to my office, so I could get some privacy and my coworkers wouldn't be able to overhear my conversation. The nurse first told me the chromosomes were normal and then asked if I wanted to know the sex. I had to know. I'm not a stick-my-head-in-the-sand type of person. Even if the information wasn't particularly helpful, I needed to know. It was a chromosomally normal *girl*. It took everything I had not to sob loudly into the phone.

Not only did we lose our baby, we lost a healthy baby. If the baby had been chromosomally abnormal or had some type of genetic defect, our loss may have been a bit easier to swallow. Still sad and devastating, but it would have made the emergency room doctor's speech about *God's Plan* make more sense. But no, my body had decided to abort a healthy, thriving baby girl.

Our reproductive doctor didn't seem too concerned. He was extremely sorry for our loss, but essentially labeled it as a random act and was hopeful that our next pregnancy would fair better. Our *next pregnancy*. This was when I truly began to despise those *assumption comments*. If we could live our life based on *assumptions*, then I should have been a mother nearly three years ago. Or I shouldn't have lost a baby at the twelve-week mark—the *assumed safe zone*. *Assuming* I wouldn't have any issues in the future wasn't an *assumption* I was comfortable with.

***

6: BABY SHOWER

Ashley, Amy's Best Friend from College

"April Showers bring May babies"—Pretty cheesy theme for a baby shower, but no one would appreciate the corniness more than Amy. Amy had always gotten my sense of humor- we were two peas in a pod. To be honest, planning a baby shower for her was always something I promised I would do- but never truly felt I would have the opportunity to do it. It was always a far out promise I would make when something horrific happened during her pregnancies. Next time Amy, next time. I'll plan the biggest, baddest baby shower ever - next time. I could hardly believe that "next time" had actually come. Although, let's be honest- I wasn't quite convinced something horrific wouldn't happen at any given point. Honest to God, I even hated to begin planning it. Would this jinx it? It seemed that having a baby shower made the baby even more real. What am I talking about? Nothing made any sense when it came to Amy and her pregnancies. All I knew, was no one on this earth deserved a baby more than Amy did, and if it was the only thing I did right that year- I would host the best baby shower ever.

A few days after we scheduled our C-section, I eagerly awaited my very first baby shower. I decided to have a baby shower while still pregnant instead of waiting until after the baby was born. This was a big decision for me, mostly because having a baby shower during pregnancy would insinuate to the world that I assumed this baby would arrive safely. That was a big no-no for me. *Sorry God, please don't curse me.* Conversely, I just couldn't shake the dream of my baby shower occurring while I was still pregnant and rocking a nice big baby bump.

I anxiously got dressed for my shower and carefully selected a bold print maternity dress with cap-sleeves. I accentuated my round bump by adding a thick black leather belt notched tightly at the empire waste line. I looked good, I felt good, and I was ready. Before I got into my car I had a quick and private conversation with my baby-to-be.

"Okay sweetie, you behave in there, okay? Mommy is going to be very busy talking and opening gifts. We're going to attempt to celebrate your impending arrival. So if you could just wiggle and kick and let me know you're doing alright in there, it would really help Mommy feel better and enjoy her day, got it?"

I, of course, received no response. My baby was not the type to be manipulated or guilted into anything on command. I could already tell she'd be one of those kids that would march to the beat of her own drum. The prospect of my baby having her own little personality, already thrilled me.

My friend Kristen hosted the shower at her house.

She just had a baby herself, about three weeks prior to the shower. I was concerned she might not have been up to hosting it for me, but she was on board and eager to be a part of the day.

Kristen and I had a special bond because we'd both lost babies. Her son, Christian, was diagnosed with a chromosomal birth defect called Trisomy 13 when she was twenty-three weeks pregnant. Trisomy 13 was a fatal condition for the baby and Kristen was devastated when she found out.

Since I had already suffered multiple losses myself, I was brokenhearted for her and her husband. I wanted so badly to be there for her in any way she needed. We sat quietly on either end of their large sectional couch. She told me I was the first one that called her a mother during her time of loss, and those words were what she so desperately needed to hear.

I marveled at how brave Kristen was. Her daughter, Harper, was only three weeks old and when we were out in public together and people asked how many children she had, she proudly stated she had two. The typical follow up question was always how old they were. She would smile softly and tell them her first son passed away, and her daughter is a few weeks old. She stated it so calmly—with pride! It blew my mind.

I wished that I had the courage to tell anyone and everyone that I had five angel babies in heaven. It would give me a sense of validation and authenticate the lives of my precious babies I gave birth to. They didn't deserve to be swept under the rug and forgotten because they didn't live for a given period of time. I carried those precious peanuts collectively for thirty-eight weeks. That deserved some recognition. I knew what it was like to be pregnant, but whenever other women would talk about the joys and challenges of pregnancy, I didn't feel I could offer any input, because I had nothing to show for mine. And surely if I would offer input, they would look at me with sad eyes, reminding everybody in the room that I'm a *habitual aborter.* At least, that's what my medical record calls me. *Nice, huh?* So instead of making comments about my experiences, I walked around with a black cloud looming over me. My eyes were always just a tiny bit strained because I had lived through horrors no one should have to endure.

As I walked into Kristen's house, I was amazed at the transformation. It had been baby-fied, times ten. Large pastel colored tissue-paper balls hung from the ceiling, streamers had been run alongside the granite counter top bar, cardboard cutout letters were displayed on the counter, spelling *baby* and some game stations had been set up along the bar top. As I looked around, my eyes zeroed in on the coat closet by the entrance and I saw a giant poster of a 3D ultrasound picture of my baby girl.

I looked to my friend Ashley, who'd helped Kristen

throw the shower and said, "Ashley, you didn't! Oh my gosh." I stopped myself because my eyes had filled with tears. To see my baby so big on a poster right before my eyes had made this whole day feel real. I had never been far enough along in any pregnancy to warrant having a baby shower. So this day felt like a legitimate cause for *hope*. We were in uncharted waters and I was starting to believe that things might actually turn out differently. My mind finally settled in on the amazing thought that this was my very first baby shower. Two of my wonderful friends gave all their effort to make the day genuine and personal. I was touched.

Ashley looked at me with her wide, clear blue eyes and said, "What?"

I gave her a knowing smile and said, "That's why you wanted me to email you the ultrasound picture, instead of texting it, like usual."

"Oh Ame-Dogger," she said with a teasing smile on her face.

I smiled proudly back at her and replied, "Ash-Dogger."

We gave each other a cheesy ear-to-ear smiling hug. Ashley was one of my favorite friends. I met her in college. She had striking black hair and ocean-blue eyes that were enough to make me look twice. When I figured out her sense of humor was as weird, random, and crude as mine, I knew we'd be fast friends.

Kristen came over and gave me a big hug too. "You like it?" she asked, nervously scrunching the back of her naturally curly, short blonde hair.

"I love it, Kristen," I said while I affectionately squeezed her arm to my side. "Everything looks so nice. I can't believe everything you guys did."

"Happy to do it, love," she said as she nudged her shoulder into mine playfully.

In no time at all, I had settled in. Ashley and Kristen had requested a list of all my favorite foods. Since I was in love with all things appetizer related, we had a lot of snack items. It was delicious. The shower consisted of all of my closest girlfriends, my two sisters and our mom. I couldn't believe it was all for me. As I sipped on some red fruity punch, I could feel our little baby moving around in my belly pretty consistently, which only added to my already glowing smile.

"Amy, I think you should start opening gifts now," Ashley said.

I was surprised how much time had already gone by. Ashley's adorable six-year-old niece gladly sidled up next to me, ready and willing to help open every last present. I made tons of awkward comments about everything I opened, mostly because I had no clue how to use the majority of it.

"More swaddle blankets! Cool, I'm sure I'll need a lot of them," I stated self-consciously. The other moms in the room probably knew I had no idea what I was talking about.

Before I knew it, I was staring at a huge pile of baby stuff. Everybody was chatting away as they nibbled on cupcakes. I looked around at all the happy faces and felt honored that all of those people were there to shower me. At last, *I* had a baby shower.

I cleared my throat and stood up in front of everyone as I held my pink paper cup of punch, "I just want to take this moment to thank you all for being here right now—" I paused as my smile turned pained and my chin trembled. "It's been a long, tough road for me and Kevin. I still can't believe most of it." As I continued, I saw the tension in the room mounting as if the earth had stopped. A room full of loved ones with teary eyes on baited breath waiting for what I would say next.

"You've all been there with us, through everything. I'm sure a lot of you were starting to run out of things to say." I laughed pitifully as the room stayed utterly silent. "But we're doing our best to get this little one here safely," I said as I rubbed my belly with my free hand. "I'm freaked out, like all of the time. I'm praying like crazy and I know you all are too. So thank you all for being my friends, my family, my support, and my lifeline. I need you all so very much and I'm so happy that I finally get to have my very own baby shower. This is a very, very big deal. Thanks again, and cheers."

The room collectively let out the huge breath they'd all been holding and sipped their punch as they allowed themselves to smile. The women in that room knew about every one of my losses. They were just as happy as I was that this was finally happening.

Kristen came over and gave me a big hug as everyone talked and looked through the gifts again. "Ugh. You've got me crying my eyes out over here! Warn me before you say that kind of stuff, will ya?" She laughed at me while she gently rubbed my back.

I swiped my hand under both my eyes and let out a sigh, "Well, I meant it. I knew I wanted to say something because this is a big moment for me, you know?"

"Yes, we know. None of us could be happier for you. I'm as excited and happy for you to have your baby as I was for me to have mine. And I really, truly mean that."

I briefly laughed as the magnitude of what her statement meant set in. It baffled me that she cared about my pregnancy as much as her own. It showed how watching a dear friend go through heartache after heartache, took its toll on the friendship. How does one tell a friend who's lost five babies that things would be okay? How could they be there for me through that? That must have been stressful.

After our first miscarriage, the advice was all the same…

Don't worry.

These things happen.

I've had a miscarriage too.

Your day will come.

God's plan.

The next one will work out just fine.

After the second miscarriage, I saw seeds of doubt on the faces of my friends and family. I knew they wondered if something more serious was going on. But once I had three in a row, it was downright pathetic. People didn't know what to say to me. All I could see in their faces was sympathy. I watched as the glimmer of optimism they used to have for me, turned into doubt. The reality that there could be no baby sunk in as I saw them all begin to lose *hope*.

***

7: SECOND TIME'S THE CHARM

Abby, Amy's Sister

Learning my sister had yet another miscarriage broke my heart. Questions ran through my mind. Why them? Why again? How can I help them get through something as tough as losing these precious babies they wanted so badly? Nothing I said could console a grieving parent. However, with Amy & Kevin, words weren't needed. Throughout their entire journey, they kept their faith, and most importantly, hope.

Our second pregnancy came rather quickly. We were over the moon. After our first loss, I went back to my reproductive endocrinologist, devastated over my turn of events and desperate to start trying again. If getting pregnant again was going to take another three years, I wanted to get the show on the road.

My RE agreed that we should do the same drugs and protocol that got me pregnant the first time. It amazingly worked on the first try. I felt my heart healing itself already.

The pregnancy proved to be a bit more stressful because I bled and spotted quite a bit. More than I had with my first pregnancy. There was a reason for it this time. They called it a subchorionic hemorrhage, which was a pocket of blood that formed inside my uterus. They said they knew it could be a little scary, but often times, things turned out okay. I had a few bad bleeding episodes, but they would rush me in for an ultrasound and find the baby growing as it should. The heart rate was always perfect. It was something I'd have to learn to deal with.

My anxiety level raised as the twelve-week mark neared. Coincidentally, the day the pregnancy hit the scary twelve-week mark, was also the original due date of my first miscarriage. I'd be lying if I said I hadn't thought it was a bad omen. Sure enough, when I hit twelve weeks pregnant—the shit hit the fan.

I was working at my office, sitting in one of those rolling big, black, leather office chairs with a high back and armrests. I had to pee. As I got up, I felt a small hitching sensation in my vaginal area and then a huge gush of fluid poured out of my vagina. It felt like the equivalent of a gallon of liquid had gushed out in a matter of seconds. My instincts told me to sit back down and put pressure on the source to stop it from leaking down my legs and spilling all over. As I sat down, I squeezed my thighs together to prevent more gushing but it felt like there was a lot more wanting to get out. One look at my lap and I saw dark red blood covered the entire crotch, butt, and thighs of my jeans.

I was trembling and unsure of what I should do. All I knew for sure was that I couldn't get up. I grabbed my cell phone and called Kevin. "Babe, it's me. I'm bleeding badly. It's everywhere," I sobbed.

"Where are you?" he asked, panic stricken.

"I'm at my desk at work. I need you to bring me clothes. Hurry," I said, shakily. "I'm going to call the doctor, just get here as fast as you can with some clothes."

Poor Kevin. I can't imagine what a shitty drive that was for him to go home, find my clothes and rush to my office.

I grabbed my office phone and paged Becky—no answer. My next thought was Judy. She was an elderly lady in the office. She was ninety pounds soaking wet but nice in a fiery, sassy kind of way. I always thought of her as being a little rough around the edges. She'd spent most of her life smoking and drinking Budweiser.

The phone beeped three times and my voice was live in her room. "Judy?"

"Yeeees," she sang back.

"This is Amy, I need you to come into my office right away. Can you hurry?" I pleaded.

"Okay," she said sounding a bit confused.

She came in a moment later with a flash of irritation on her face, possibly because she had been given an order so abruptly.

"I need paper towels, and fast," I cried.

She looked a little confused and rushed back out of the door and into the break room for our office stash.

She reentered my office with an entire roll of paper towel. More blood seeped out and spilled off the sides of my chair onto the plastic floor mat my wheelie office chair sat on. I saw her reaction set in. She didn't look squeamish or scared, just assessing.

I stuffed the paper towels under my butt without getting up so the blood I felt waiting to burst out wouldn't. I blurted out suddenly, "I'm pregnant and I don't know what's going on. It just keeps coming out."

She looked stunned and scared for a split second, but immediately masked her features back to neutral and went into disaster mode. She dropped down onto her hands and knees and wiped the blood that was pouring out of my body off the floor with fresh paper towels. *This blood was coming from where my baby was!* "We need to get you to the bathroom to get you cleaned up," she said in her scratchy smoker's voice.

"I don't think I can get up, Judy. It feels like there's tons more that wants to come out if I move."

Without another word, her tiny little frame pushed my chair toward my back office door. There was a men's bathroom back there that was much closer than the women's. She finessed me over the lip of the doorframe and we were in the hallway. I glanced in either direction down the long hallway and prayed to God nobody walked by.

It occurred to me that some people might think bleeding large quantities like this would require a 911 call. Since I still had my wits about me and knew this was just another pregnancy complication, the expense of a ride in an ambulance didn't seem necessary. I just knew I needed to get myself cleaned up and over to the hospital as soon as possible.

As she got me to the bathroom door, Kevin walked in looking flustered and scared. He saw me sitting in my office chair and his eyes looked like they'd seen a ghost. He quickly helped me up and into the bathroom. We left Judy and the bloody chair in the hallway.

As soon as he shut the door I lost it. "It's happening again, Kevin. There's blood everywhere!" I screeched.

He helped me to the toilet and pulled my blood-soaked jeans down my legs.

"It's going to be okay. We'll get you changed and over to the doctor's office."

I sat on the toilet, shaking uncontrollably as I looked at him, fearfully. "It feels like something big needs to come out." Then suddenly, plop. I spread my legs and looked down into the toilet and saw a blood clot the size of a grapefruit.

Nearly hysterical, I stood and yelled, "Is that our baby?"

He bent over and looked at the bloody mass, "No, I don't think so, it's just blood. It's just blood."

"We need to take it with us, just in case," I said.

Kevin assured me it wasn't the baby, so I let him flush it down the toilet. For me, the most important thing of all my miscarriages was finding out why. If I could bring my baby into the hospital, they could grow the cells out and count the chromosomes so I would know if it was a chromosome abnormality. I could also find out the sex of the baby.

After I was cleaned up, we called the doctor. They were able to get us straight to ultrasound, so we could bypass the emergency room. We walked out of the bathroom and Judy was there, cleaning my chair. My heart broke looking at her tiny body wiping and scrubbing the mess that came from me.

"No, please Judy! You don't have to do that," I exclaimed pleadingly, tears overrunning my eyes.

She looked up at me with a determined expression, "Not another word, you get to the hospital and I'll take care of everything else." She resumed scrubbing, still looking at me.

I looked at her, horrified. She gave me the look a stern mother would that effectively ended our disagreement. I knew there was still a bloody scene to be dealt with in my office but there was nothing Kevin or I could do in that moment.

When we got into the ultrasound room, the tech told me to take off my pants and get on the exam table. I told her I would leak blood all over because it was pouring out of me. "That's okay, we've seen it before." I wasn't too sure they had. I thought she was just being nice. Maybe the ER had seen bloody shows like it, but I doubted those ultrasound rooms were equipped to deal with emergency traumas like this. I felt the blood running down my butt-crack as my feet were up in the stirrups.

The tech pushed the probe in and amazingly, after losing what felt like a gallon or more of blood and passing a grapefruit sized clot, my baby was still in there with the heart still beating. The doctor walked in and explained that it could go either way at this point. All we could do was get some rest and wait.

Nervously, we went home. Shock and terror was still streaked across our faces, alongside dried tears. The next day there was off and on bleeding. I dared myself to hope we could get through this rough patch.

That night, the bleeding suddenly increased. We hurried to the emergency room. I had lost a lot of blood, but the baby was still in there. I was a mess. The ER doctor told us to expect to lose the baby because my cervix was wide open and it was only a matter of time. I was heartbroken and focused on the clotting blood that was coming out of me. The blood kept sticking inside my vagina and I felt like if I just pushed real hard it would all release and I would feel so much better. I knew that pushing while I was trying to save my baby was the last thing I wanted to do. The nurse came in and discharged me. As she walked out, I told Kevin I couldn't get dressed until this blood got out of me. Kevin helped me to the bathroom and I tried desperately to wipe out the large clots that were forming and sticking. At one point, I put myself back on the exam table and had Kevin help me pull some of the clots out. It was awful. I'm sure that's an image he never expected to see with his wife, but Kevin loved me unconditionally, so if this was something I needed done, he wasn't about to hesitate.

The next day, at twelve weeks and two days pregnant, I had a follow up appointment with my doctor and the baby was still in there, heartbeat drumming away. The doctor said there was still a chance this baby could make it. We were on an emotional rollercoaster of hope and despair.

That night, while lying in bed, I felt heavy cramps. I tried to sleep with pregnancy-safe pain meds that I had been prescribed, but waves of cramps kept coming and going. They woke me every ten minutes or so and I would cry out. Kevin held me until the cramps subsided and then I'd sleep again for another ten minutes, until the next onslaught hit me. This went on for a couple of hours. I wasn't aware I was having contractions. I didn't know that was possible with a twelve-week pregnancy.

Around midnight, I went into the bathroom to pee as I had hoped to relieve the pressure I felt in my lower belly. Kevin followed along with his hand gently caressing my back, to help soothe some of my pain. He followed me everywhere during those difficult days. Thankfully, his work understood that he needed time off so he could be home with me.

As soon as I sat down, blood poured into the toilet. I was used to blood at this point because of the subchorionic hemorrhage. I had what felt like a full flow period of blood soaking pads every three to four hours throughout this entire pregnancy. But this was different.

I looked up to Kevin for answers I knew he wouldn't have, "Grab me a dish or something to catch any tissue that might come out. This is bad, Kevin!"

Kevin disappeared for a moment and came back with clear, rectangular Tupperware. "Here," he said handing me the dish.

A second later I felt something big coming, something uncomfortable and painful. Suddenly, it passed through my vaginal walls and I quickly darted the Tupperware between my legs.

"Ouch, that hurt!" I cried out. It was the first time that something physically hurt when it came out. All of the other clots and blood I had passed prior to that never caused pain. Not even the grapefruit. This felt like a solid mass with pointy edges or something.

A strange squealing sound came from my throat as I caught it. I knew it was our baby. There was a sac of some sort around it and a lot of blood and small clots.

"This is the baby, Kevin!" I blurted, looking up to him in complete agony.

His disturbed expression told me he had no clue what to say back. Blood continued to stream out of me into the toilet like a faucet. It sounded like I was peeing.

"Go get the Doppler so I can see if there's still a heartbeat!" I screamed. I was in no mood for manners. I was in the middle of hell; forgive me for not saying *please*.

My fetal heart rate monitor looked like a tiny

microphone attached to a small speaker. I clambered off the toilet and lied down on the cool, hard bathroom tile next to my bloody clothes. I felt the blood continuing to leak out of me as it pooled onto the floor below my bottom. I pressed the Doppler head to my lower abdomen while I prayed I was wrong and would hear the heartbeat.

When I didn't pick anything up, I declared, "I can't find it Kevin. That was the baby, I'm sure of it. We need to get to the ER. Go find me some clothes."

At that point, I was in survivor mode. I was emotional and tearful, but detached and only thinking about what needed to be done so I was barking orders like a drill sergeant.

Kevin brought me fresh clothes but there was so much blood coming out of me, I had to stuff a thick bath towel between my legs as a pad.

As I was lying on my back, Kevin slipped my feet through the legs of my grey sweat pants. "You're going to have to put a towel on the seat in the car too. I don't want to get blood everywhere," I told him while I felt blood rush in my ears. "And put a lid on that Tupperware and set it inside a brown paper bag."

He helped me stand and ran out of the bathroom to dutifully follow my instructions. I placed my hands on the vanity and looked at myself in the mirror. The room spun as I turned to exit the bathroom. I felt lightheaded so I leaned my hands on the wall for support. It was like the room was rocking back and forth. I wasn't sure I'd make it to the car, but I had to try. I realized I'd lost too much blood and that was why I was feeling like this. I didn't have time to contemplate, I knew we had to get to the hospital.

Kevin had the brown paper bag clasped tightly in his hand and was rushing around frantically to get things ready to go. I weakly folded myself into the car.

When we got to the ER, I must have looked horrible because they rushed right over to me in the car with a wheelchair. I was taken right back without being forced to sit in the waiting room.

The doctor came in and we told him what happened. He peered into the brown paper bag and removed the clear Tupperware container. He looked at it briefly and said that he wanted to order an ultrasound.

"Is that the baby?" I asked him expectantly.

His expression was severe, "Yes, I believe so, but we really should do an ultrasound to confirm."

An ultrasound showed that we did in fact lose the baby and it was sitting in the Tupperware. I felt a small moment of relief when they said I'd miscarried, *my agony was finally over.* For two days I'd bled and clotted, gushed and leaked. It was a living nightmare. The blood kept pouring out as they informed us of the situation.

The ER doctor said they had to do an emergency D&C to stop the bleeding and they would need to put me under. We were never given an offer to see the baby or say goodbye, mostly because there wasn't time. I didn't think I wanted to see it again anyway. I got a glimpse of it when it came out of me and it didn't look like something I wanted a visual memory of. I assumed the baby just ended up with our first baby. I guess I was okay with that, because I felt like they'd be together.

When I woke up from surgery, the doctor told Kevin that they were very close to doing a blood transfusion because my hemoglobin was incredibly low due to all of the blood I had lost the past few days. He said they didn't because I was young and strong, and it would be better for me to bring it back up on my own because blood transfusions carry their own risks, like infection, allergic reactions, etc. He explained I would be severely anemic for three to four months while my body tried to right itself. He also stated the symptoms would make me tired all the time and cause frequent headaches. It would be a tough few months.

Once again, Kevin and I left the emergency room, empty-handed. My body rid itself of the contents of my baby, restoring itself back to where it was comfortable. Not pregnant.

8: JEALOUSY

Amber, Amy's Older Sister

I can blink and I am pregnant—that is always what I used to brag about to people. Although, not literally true, getting pregnant is definitely not a difficult task for me. So, after my sister suffered miscarriage after miscarriage and I watched it all—I dreaded having to tell her I was pregnant with my second child. How could I expect someone who had lost so much, to be happy for me when I already had what she so desperately wanted?

After the second miscarriage, Kevin and I decided to take a break. It was such a horrific, graphic, and horrendous experience. We needed time to heal. Thankfully, my sister had cleaned up the mess prior to us coming home from the hospital. Judy had cleaned my chair and office. There were no traces of the scene when I got to work. It was humbling to think of how many people had to clean up my blood.

For some reason, I wasn't immediately devastated with this miscarriage the way I was for my first. In fact, as previously mentioned, I felt a sense of relief when it was over. It had been so incredibly stressful with the multiple bleeding episodes. The ups and downs were so hard to handle as we had to wonder if the baby would hang in there.

In addition, I was due to be a bridesmaid in three different weddings that summer for my younger sister Abby, and my two best friends, Ashley and Desiree. The timing of this pregnancy wasn't ideal for those weddings. Had the pregnancy worked out, I would have been in my third trimester for all three weddings. I would have been thirty-six weeks along before the last wedding came around in October. But I was so desperate to be pregnant that every month counted. The thought of delaying our attempts at conception because of other people's life events seemed unfeasible to me. Kevin and I had been trying for over three years. Who knew how long it would take to conceive the next baby? If destiny had me due for a few BFN—*Big Fat Negative* cycles of trying, I wanted to get them under my belt and out of the way and not delayed for scheduling purposes. At that point in our journey, everything seemed urgent. But deep down I knew I wouldn't be pregnant anyway. Something bad would happen. It always did.

My grief didn't subside for long. The chromosome results of the baby were inconclusive. Visually they noted the baby had appeared normal. I knew in my heart, *this one was healthy too.* To top things off, I had developed a superficial clot in my right calf. Most likely a result of being postpartum and postoperative, but it was still added to my very extensive list of medical issues.

Over the next six months I grew angrier and more resentful than ever. Unfortunately, Kevin had to take the brunt of most of it, which was a real strain on our marriage. In my eyes, he couldn't do anything right.

One really ridiculous fight we got in was over hanging out with his friends instead of mine. Kevin wanted to invite his friend, Shaun, up to a concert in our town. He thought I could hang out with Shaun's wife, Denise, while they were gone. Denise was pregnant with their second child and that did *not* sound like my idea of fun.

When I told Kevin I didn't want to hang out with Denise, he got angry because he said I always hung out with my friend, Linsey, and she was pregnant too so it shouldn't be any different.

It was a huge blowout fight that involved me storming out of the house to drive around for an hour just to get away from him. I knew it didn't entirely make sense, but it was just easier hanging out with *my* pregnant friends than his. Not to mention, Linsey had suffered a miscarriage before she achieved this pregnancy, so I connected with her on that level.

At that time in my life, if I was going to hang out with someone that was pregnant, I needed to have a close connection with that person, or I was completely miserable. Since I was close to Linsey, it didn't bother me as much that she was big and pregnant. I knew it wasn't fair, but that was my rationalization.

Kevin couldn't understand that no matter how hard I tried to explain it to him. He's just too much of a nice guy that he couldn't fathom how hanging out with certain people might be difficult for me. That's why his nice-guy routine got old at times. He couldn't understand *me*. It was a dark time for us.

At one point we discussed couples therapy, but that just spurred more fights. Kevin was horribly against it. He felt that couples therapy carried a bad stigma, and showed weakness in him as a man, and in our marriage.

Part of my irritability was due to the twenty-four/seven headaches caused by the anemia. I felt run down and tired all day, every day. Work was really difficult and I constantly had people tell me that I looked pale or sickly. Also, I was postpartum, so my hormone levels were plummeting from the previous pregnancy state that my body was in.

The majority of my prickliness was plainly because our life sucked. I had gained at least twenty pounds since we began our journey of trying to conceive. I was unhappy with my body and our situation. *Two miscarriages in a row, are you kidding me?*

Furthermore, it seemed that everywhere I looked, pregnant women surrounded me. Every time I miscarried, someone close to me was pregnant. So I had to swallow that shit-sandwich and put on my happy face whenever there was a baby shower or birth.

I remember after one of my losses, my older sister pulled me aside in my parents' laundry room one weekend when we were home visiting. She wanted to warn me that they were going to announce to Mom and Dad that they were pregnant with baby number two. The pitiful and sorrowful look on her face that night made me feel pathetic. However, for some reason, it was easier to handle my sister's pregnancy than others. Most likely, it was because my sister was older than me, so it just seemed appropriate for her to be having babies.

Moreover, I think I had a closer, motherly connection with her two boys. We were related by blood. There was a comfort level with my nephews that I didn't have with anyone else's children. Not to mention my four-year-old nephew, Evan, looked a lot like me. I was proud of him and latched onto that connection because it was the closest thing I had to a baby of my own.

Nonetheless, her news still hurt. I smiled brightly at her and feigned excitement. Shortly thereafter, I ran into the bathroom to conceal my outburst from everyone's sympathetic glances.

I consequently became obsessed with asking my friends and family if they were pregnant. I was desperate to know. It felt like a form of emotional cutting. I just couldn't help myself. I incessantly asked people before they had the chance to tell me. I was positively a masochist but I was trying my hardest to save myself from some big, happy, surprise announcement in front of a room full of people. Even with preparation, it still stung when they would get their big moment and I had to sit there with a history of dead babies. It was like watching someone sit right in front of you and eat a big, juicy steak while you're dying of hunger.

Kevin's brother and sister-in-law also got pregnant with their second baby after our second miscarriage. We were all home visiting Kevin's parents on their family farm for the weekend. It was a small old farmhouse where everybody sat around the kitchen table drinking beer and playing cards all night. There were not a lot of places to hide. I saw my sister-in-law whispering something into the ear of their three-year-old. Her husband looked on with excitement and I knew exactly what was coming. A wave of anxiety filled my entire body. It was complete and utter torture. Heartbreaking agony. It wasn't fair how easily other couples could get pregnant.

Later that night, as the beers continued to flow at Kevin's parent's house, the subject inevitably turned to our miscarriages. Talking about it was something I loved to do because it always felt like an elephant in the room. I actually got angry when nobody addressed it or asked about it. It made me feel like nobody cared about what we went through. I knew it was an awkward topic, but for God's sake, we had lost two babies. Could no one see how hurt we were by that every day?

So once everyone had a bit of liquid courage, they weren't too insecure to broach the topic of our losses. We'd been discussing the dirty details of our most recent loss, when Kevin's brother got visibly upset and boomed out, "Why is it so difficult for you guys, and so damn easy for us? It's infuriating that you guys can't have the child you want as easily as we can. Life is not fair!"

I felt like I'd been slapped. Like a cold bucket of water had just been splashed in my face. His comment did not have the desired effect he was reaching for. He was trying to show solidarity and compassion for our situation, but all I heard was his shouting about how damn easy it was for them to get pregnant, as his newly pregnant wife sat there glowing from her new pregnancy hormones.

That was a lot of what I faced on a regular basis. People didn't understand how to talk to me. Why they thought I wanted them to tell me how easy it was for them to get pregnant was beyond me. Maybe there was no right or wrong way to talk to me about pregnancy loss? Maybe it was just a shit show and we all just had to deal with it in our own way. But seeing and hearing things related to other women's pregnancies was a daily occurrence for me.

I stared with green-eyed envy at the hugely pregnant women who bounced around without a care in the world. One time, I was at a costume party and watched a beautifully pregnant gal dancing on the dance floor. She was maybe thirty weeks pregnant. I just sat and stared with my jaw dropped as she jumped and gyrated on the dance floor. There were tons of people drinking and partying around her, but she didn't have a care in the world. She looked great and healthy and perfectly content in her pregnant form. I must have looked so pathetic sitting there in my cheesy cowboy costume, sipping on my bottle of beer and staring at her like a psychopath. All I could think to myself was that I would never be so lucky. I would never be able to have *fun* while being pregnant. If it had been me out there, I would have cramped and bled and my baby would have most likely fallen right out onto the dance floor.

I knew that was unfair. I knew there were women who exercised, jogged, worked manual labor type of jobs, went to weddings, parties, stayed up late and carried thirty-pound toddlers on top of their massive baby bumps and their babies didn't fall out. I couldn't help but judge. Deep down, I was sick with jealousy.

I wanted to kill myself after I heard a pregnant friend of a friend, simply state, "Sometimes I literally forget I'm pregnant!" *Shoot me. Please, just take a gun and put me out of my misery, like Old Yeller. If I have to hear much more of this, I'm going to turn into a rabid dog anyway.*

The issue was that we went through life thinking we'd never be fulfilled until we had children to complete our family. I had begun to resent that notion. How could I not? One day, my newly-pregnant sister-in-law posted on Facebook: *You've never experienced the magic of Christmas until you see it through your child's eyes.* I hated that comment. Hated it! I wanted to post a reply and say, *what about me?* I'm sure that would have made her squirm. How dare she assume that those of us without children don't know the meaning of Christmas? I'm one thousand percent certain that's not what she meant, and she hadn't considered my feelings, or the feelings of others who have suffered pregnancy losses when she was writing the post, but every time she got another thumbs up on her post, I was *that* much closer to flagging it as offensive.

For the first time in my life, I was trying to come to grips with the idea that I might not have kids. I was working hard to justify a life with just Kevin and myself. Twice, we had arrived at the magical twelve-week safe zone, when our risk of miscarriage had gone way down.

Twice, we got slapped in the face with the death of our babies. I wanted to give up hope. I wanted to find other ways to be happy because my heart was so broken.

As I researched, I discovered that having losses at the twelve-week mark was pretty uncommon. I was desperately looking online for other women who had twelve-week losses similar to mine. But mine were so different because it was as if I was going into labor. They weren't missed-miscarriages, where the woman doesn't realize the baby had passed away until her next ultrasound. I had twelve-week deliveries. My babies were alive, until they came out of my body. It was awful. All I needed to know was if someone out there lived through what I did and still went on to have their own baby, but I was coming up empty-handed, which was scary.

Kevin's emotional stability was questionable too. Could he stand to go through another loss as dreadful and graphic as the one we'd just had? Could he go through pulling clots of blood out from between my legs again? That is something no husband should have to do. Kevin was once the king of optimism, yet even he was showing seeds of doubt. It was heartrending. Once Kevin started having uncertainty, that's when I knew things were pretty grim for us.

As a result of the newfound fear and doubt he was expressing, I resented him even more than I had for being *Mr. Optimistic*. I felt like I was alone in the journey. I was the only one online seeking the answers to our hundreds of questions. Kevin had become increasingly frustrated with the time I spent online. The truth was, we shared a deep, dark, ugly tragedy together and instead of letting it bring us closer together, we were letting it rip us apart.

It didn't help that every time I walked into our bathroom, my mind's-eye showed me the bloody scene that we had left behind that night. I knew I would never be able to look at my bathroom floor, or my office chair, the same way. All I would see was the bloody nightmare we lived through.

I begrudged the fact that I was married because that put pressure on us to start a family. If I were single, I wouldn't have been going through any of it. My biggest worries would be clothes, going to bars and meeting people. I could be young and carefree again without knowing the issues of my reproductive organs. I started searching for jobs overseas just to fantasize about commencing a new life away from all this pain and anguish. I had no intention to leave Kevin, but I had hoped I could get him on board if a job presented itself. I just wanted to run from our current life, into a new life that didn't include memories of dead babies everywhere I went.

Fortunately, Kevin and I slowly got better, but we never operated at one-hundred-percent happy. How could anyone who'd gone through what we had, ever *truly* be happy? I focused on myself, lost some weight, got healthier and felt better. We got back into the same routine we'd been in before; working, watching movies on the couch together and hanging out with friends, preferably the ones who did not have babies. It was all a great escape from our pain. After the movie was done, or we came home from the bar, reality would settle back in and that pit in my stomach would return. I was never allowed to forget.

I walked around in life with haunting images in my head. I would go to the grocery store and gather with friends, none of whom really knew the reality of the situation I went through. I could tell them what happened, but unless they were flies on the wall that night, or I wrote a detailed book about it, they would never be able to understand. In a way, I knew I had to become closer with Kevin, because he was the only one who really knew the depths of my despair. He was the only one who had a similar perspective on life. Once we went through something so major, our views on life shifted together.

***

9: FIGHTING

Kevin, Amy's Husband

We were not always on the same page when all of our tragedies happened. One of the biggest issues was adoption. I wanted to adopt a child. Mainly because I was exhausted, worrying about all of Amy's pain and misery. This may seem selfish, but in my mind it was the one thing I knew would give us something more to love without risking Amy's health. Those miscarriages were very tough on us emotionally and physically. I was constantly worried about Amy when things went bad. Amy did consider adoption, but she would not give up until she got answers to her medical questions.
Her perseverance is what I love most about her.

Being thirty-four weeks pregnant, Kevin's sister, a photographer, had convinced us to do a maternity photoshoot. I always wanted to have pictures taken because taking pictures was a side-hobby of mine. Of course I wanted to capture the amazing body I was currently rocking.

"Babe, are you about ready?" Kevin yelled as he slumped onto the couch looking cranky and impatient.

"Yeah, I'm just getting my necklace and shoes on," I said as I walked out of the bathroom and into our bedroom, fumbling with my clasp. I quickly adjusted the full-panel maternity-jeans and slightly cringed. I was definitely achy and crampy, as usual. I always asked the doctor about it and he always replied with the same answer, "Growing pains—normal, blah blah blah." Everything looked good and the baby was growing just right, so it was just part of the stretching process.

"Ugh, Kev, my stomach really hurts!" I yelled down the hall. I sat down on the bed and pulled the maternity panel on my pants outward, away from my stomach, in attempt to find some relief from the pressure and aching.

Kevin came into the room and sat down beside me. "It's probably nothing babe, the doctor said to expect the cramping and stuff. It's no different than all of the other times you've had cramping with this one."

"How do you know, Kevin?" I snapped. "All I said is my stomach hurts. You don't know the details of how I feel. You haven't even fricken' asked."

Kevin pulled back slightly with an expression like he

had poked a grizzly bear. He replied back slowly, "Okay, I'm sorry. Does this feel a lot different? Do you think you might need to poop?"

"I don't need to poop, Kevin. I don't know what this is. I hate this so much." I rubbed my belly in a pleading manner. "I hate that I never know when something bad is going to happen and that we can't just make plans to go do something without worrying I might kill the baby," I said, feeling the ache in my throat as my emotions reached a boiling point.

Kevin stood up angrily and stared down at me in stony silence.

"Don't say that," he huffed as he raked his hands through his hair. "You say that shit and it pisses me off. You're not going to kill the baby!"

"Argh, I want this to be over," I cried. "I don't want to be afraid of my own freaking body for just one day. For one day I would like a break from feeling like any second I'm going to gush blood and it will all be over again. Just one fricken' day! You have no clue what I'm going through, Kevin. No clue at all," I sobbed and quickly lay down on my side and curled my legs up toward my belly as far as my bulge would allow.

Kevin sat back down next to me and put his hand on my hip. "You think this is easy for me? You think I don't think about what's going on with you every day? I do. I think about it a lot." Kevin's face was turning red as he reacted to my outburst.

"Not constantly!" I yelled angrily into the pillow. I pathetically struggled to push myself back up off the bed and faced him. "No way do you think about this as much as I do. My mind is always fricken' on it! I'm forever thinking about this baby. I can't turn it off because it's inside my body. There's not one second that goes by that I'm not constantly aware of being pregnant. So don't look at me and tell me you think about it all the time. You can't possibly understand what it's like to be me!"

"Okay, not constantly," Kevin replied, scratching the top of his head in exasperation. "But sometimes you act like you're the only one going through this."

"At times it feels like I am," my voice cracked. I knew I was being horrible, but I couldn't stop. The accusations may not have been accurate, but they were my feelings and I was going to express them. In that moment, I felt like I HAD to express them. The stress in my body was like a poison that needed to be expelled. Unfortunately, my husband took the brunt of it. The beauty of our marriage was that although we were sometimes awful and terrible to each other, and said mean things we would later regret, we never doubted our love for each other. I was always hardest on Kevin because he was closest to me—he would always forgive me. I never worried about his love wavering, so I couldn't help but let all my guards down and be open and raw. I was so exhausted, both emotionally and physically. I just wanted a break from being scared. Being terrified for eight agonizing months was debilitating. Not to mention the years of struggle before then.

"I don't want you to feel like you're alone," Kevin said calmly. "I want to help, but I just don't know how. That's why I wanted us to adopt so bad. It's hard to sit here and watch you go through this stuff and not be able to do anything." Kevin sighed heavily.

"Don't fricken' throw adoption in my face now, Kevin," I sneered gesturing toward my bulging stomach.

"I'm not, I'm sorry," Kevin said hurriedly. "I don't know what I'm saying. That's not what I meant." Kevin sighed again. "I just wish I knew how to help you more. I feel like I can't do anything right."

Kevin hunched his head and shoulders and rubbed his hands together nervously. I knew he didn't deserve it and I knew what he was trying to say. He just wasn't expressing himself at what I felt was the right time. I wasn't in the right frame of mind to hear him.

"Right now, Kevin, I just need you to support me," I said finally getting a grip on my emotions. "Don't minimize me or placate me. Listen to what I'm saying and take my fears seriously."

"What does placate mean?" Kevin looked over at

me, seriously, with the corners of his mouth threatening a smile. We simultaneously started laughing at each other. It was a sad, pathetic kind of laugh, but it felt good. It was a relief from the tension that had been mounting since he walked into the room.

"You're such an idiot," I said teasingly. "Let's call Megan and tell her we're going to be late so I can lie down and see if these cramps go away."

"Ok, I'll call her now," Kevin exhaled as he stood. "Are we okay?" he inquired.

"Yes, we're fine," I said and waved him off like he was being silly.

A short while after taking off my pants and lying down, I had to use the restroom. I guess Kevin was right, and I didn't mind admitting it because I was so thankful when I had a cause and effect for my cramps. The problem was that due to my history, when it came to bowel movements, they had to essentially let themselves out. There was no way I would push or strain anything out down there for fear that I'd push the baby out with it. That was a big reason why my stomach was cramping so much. I was always backed up until my body could do it all on its own, without any help from me.

After immense relief, I took one final look in the mirror and adjusted my yellow print infinity scarf around my neck. I felt better and looked good. The scarf contrasted nicely with my teal colored batwing top.

I peeked out of the bathroom door while I adjusted my jewelry. Kevin was sitting in the living room, "Why aren't your shoes on? You're seriously sitting here waiting for me and you're not even ready to go? Come on," I said frustrated.

Kevin jumped up off the couch searching around for his shoes. "I didn't know how long you would be."

"You just asked me," I said as I made my way to the doorway that entered into our garage. "So now I'm ready and we're waiting on you."

Getting out the door was always such an ordeal for us. Granted, I was a female and I did take longer to get ready, but Kevin never thought ahead. He was always halfway ready and sitting around waiting until I was ready and then acted surprised when it was time to leave.

As we pulled up to our shooting location, I was trying to envision various poses we could do. Definitely no bare-belly shots. Thin red stripes were beginning to develop on the lower part of my belly. I wasn't one of the lucky ones that never got stretch marks. Those women who could bare all in a bikini or a wispy piece of blowing fabric while thirty-plus weeks pregnant, could just suck it! The truth was, I wasn't wild about my bare belly prior to pregnancy and I sure as hell wasn't wild about it now. In fact, aside from the stretch marks, pregnancy may have improved my belly some because it made it tighter.

The area we took pictures in was behind an artsy, quaint, outdoor strip mall. The back of the mall looked very industrial and had a huge loading dock area with rear entrances for the various shops and boutiques. I had done shoots there before, so I knew there were a lot of unique options there.

We got out of our car just as my coworker, Becky, pulled up. I had asked her to come along and help pose us and adjust our clothes. I knew from experience that an assistant on a photo-shoot is always nice and she just loved being involved in anything fun like this.

Kevin's younger sister, Megan, appeared around the corner of the upper-level loading area. "Hey guys, how's it going?" she said excitedly.

"Hey, Megan. It's going good! You like this spot okay?" I asked as I slammed the car door shut.

"Oh yeah, this is great. There are some cool graffiti murals we could shoot in front of if you're okay with that," she said as she pushed back her medium length blonde hair.

"Sounds perfect," I said as we made our way over to the spot.

I handed Becky the bag of props we had brought along. One prop was a little red wagon that said *It's a Girl* on the side, in bold white letters, leftover from my baby shower. Next to that, was a special onesie I wanted for a shot later.

Megan attempted to delicately pose my not so flexible body. And poor Kevin was not good with pictures. One eye always closed a little and he looked awkward in every pose. About halfway through the shoot, Megan and Becky quit being polite with their words and simply told Kevin to smile better.

But overall, the shoot was good. I felt like I couldn't stop smiling through all of it even if I wanted to. We were having fun for once. I danced like a loon and used my big protruding belly as a prop. I'm sure we looked like fools, but we were laughing the whole time. We were being our non-traditional selves. *We were being us.*

After a few silly shots, I switched my shirt to a dark brown top with gold sequins on the neckline. I pulled my hair back into a low-slung ponytail. I asked Becky to hand me the bag of props. I pulled out a tiny white onesie with pink lettering embroidered on the front that said *Fertility Drugs Rock.* This was a very sweet gift I had received from Ashley at my baby shower. I loved it. It was so me.

I was never secretive about my fertility treatments. I think some women feel like less of a woman if they need fertility treatments, but I completely disagree with that thought process. There was no shame in needing some assistance to have a baby. I was making a life for goodness sake. It didn't matter how it was made. I would shout it from a mountaintop that my daughter was a product of gonadotropins, fertility injections that helped me grow my follicles…a.k.a. eggs. Because darn it, I was proud. I thought more women should speak out about their fertility struggles because there were women out there going through it privately. It was a difficult process to go through, so I could only imagine what it would be like to go through it truly alone.

After doing a cheesy thumbs-up pose with the special onesie draped over my big belly, I looked over at Megan. She had her head down as she looked through the photos. "Hey Meg, I want to get some shots with the gold rings near my belly and our hands clasped around them or something. Can we try that?"

"Absolutely!" she answered eagerly.

Those five gold rings meant a lot to me. They represented each of my angel babies; my losses and my nightmares. They were beautiful and tragic all at the same time. I never wanted to forget them. I loved wearing a constant reminder of them. They were looped through an old leather-strap necklace that I found buried in an old jewelry box from my childhood. They hung short around my neck. I often grabbed ahold of the tiny rings throughout the day and rubbed each one individually. It felt like I was giving a gentle squeeze to my babies the only way I could. It definitely didn't replace a kiss on a peach fuzzed head, or buzzing my lips on their bellies, but it was all I had.

I was thankful to have a symbol of them to wear proudly everyday. I felt like it validated their lives and reminded those close to me that I still thought about my babies, every day.

At times they were difficult to wear. I would be at a party and someone that didn't know me would ask about the meaning behind them. Even though I was proud to wear them, it was difficult being transported back to the grieving mother mode when I was in a room full of people drinking beer. It definitely changed the mood I was in, that was for sure.

There was a time when we were at my in-laws again, all sitting around their big kitchen table, drinking beer and playing cards. My niece was sitting on my lap facing me, playing with the gold rings. She was only three at the time so I didn't think she knew anything about them and she blurted out, "Are these for your dead babies?"

Everyone froze. I was not prepared for such a question, but somehow I managed to tell her something about having the gold rings so I could remember them forever. I eventually scooted her off my lap and ran into the bathroom to hide my tears from everyone's watchful eyes. I'd never stop wearing my gold rings; they were a part of me. But to have them brought up in random conversation still jarred me at times.

I received the gold rings on December twelfth of 2010 from the hospital after I suffered my third miscarriage. We had lost twins that time.

***

10: DE JA VU X2

Amy, Registered Nurse

At the beginning of my shift, I was told my assignment would be a patient coming up from the ER that was likely experiencing a loss. I, sadly, had worked with a lot of families who went through this and I always prayed before going into the room. "Lord, help me find the right words and actions to help this family get through these moments. Please bring peace upon them and wrap your loving arms around them and their baby." This day was no different. Everything happened so quickly. Her fourteen-week-old baby came out very suddenly and when I went to clean the baby up, I noticed the twin they had lost at nine weeks was there, grasping onto the fourteen-week baby. It was as if it was being embraced by its twin. How amazing. The nine-week baby was so perfectly formed; fingers, toes, arms, legs, eye buds. It was one of the most eye-opening experiences in my career.

How true it is that 'A person's a person, no matter how small.'

Losing two singleton pregnancies was hard enough. But when I lost my twins in my third pregnancy, I didn't know if it could get any worse.

Kevin and I had taken a long break from trying to conceive after our second miscarriage. We got through two of the weddings I was in and decided we were ready to try again. I had lost twenty-five pounds. I was doing acupuncture and I felt great. Acupuncture was a new thing for me but I was willing to try since Western medicine hadn't been a big help to me thus far. It was expensive because my insurance wouldn't cover it, but if it would help get my baby into the world safely, that was all that mattered.

We decided to go back to my reproductive endocrinologist and do the same medicine protocol we had done all the times before. He would also add Lovenox blood thinners twice a day due to my clot history and daily Progesterone in Oil shots per my request. I had read a lot on progesterone and thought the shots could help. All of these were self administered drugs. I went home, did all my shots at the designated times, came in for regular ultrasounds to track the growth of my follicles and did the baby dance when they told us to. Sure enough, we got pregnant.

The blood results showed that my HCG numbers were coming back higher than my two pregnancies before that. HCG is known as the pregnancy hormone and it's how the doctors confirmed my pregnancy via a blood test. It's also the hormone that showed up on the take home pregnancy tests. In normal pregnancies, they like to see the HCG number double every two days. My first few tests were tripling, which sometimes indicated twins or triplets, so we were extra nervous to get the first ultrasound.

About a week later after the first blood tests confirmed I was pregnant, I started cramping. It was still too early for the pregnancy to be confirmed on an ultrasound, so instead, they rechecked my HCG numbers. The numbers were going up, but they weren't doubling or tripling like they initially had been.

At that time, Kevin and I were preparing to leave for Kansas City because my childhood best friend, Desiree, was getting married and I was her maid of honor. However, I was not feeling right at all. The cramps were constant. I was frequently Googling my symptoms, convinced I had internal bleeding. My gut was telling me it was an ectopic pregnancy, a pregnancy located in a fallopian tube. It's very dangerous and a huge cause for concern. An ectopic pregnancy would cause my tube to rupture, which would have consequently caused me to bleed out, lose a tube, develop an infection, or worse. It definitely wouldn't have been good for my fertility either.

We decided to take a trip to the emergency room before we left for Kansas City to check on things and hopefully get some answers about the abdominal pain. I was four weeks pregnant at the time. They did an ultrasound just in case they could see anything, however, whatever was in there was still too small to see. The emergency room doctor called my RE to see what he thought of my situation. My RE advised me not to travel to the wedding, despite knowing that I was the maid of honor. I was stunned. There was no way I could miss my best friend's wedding! We'd been friends ever since we were babies, so I ignored his advice.

It was a five-hour car ride to Kansas City and I knew I wasn't going to be comfortable. Luckily, the nurse gave me pain pills to help get me through the weekend so I would make it down the aisle without hunching over in pain. Kevin and I made sure we knew where the nearest hospitals were in case things took a turn for the worse.

I knew the odds of miscarrying were high. It was my third pregnancy and had already started off horribly. I was barely pregnant at that point, nothing had shown up on the ultrasound, so if I were to miscarry, it would be like getting my period a week or two late. The fact was, if I started bailing on family functions, weddings, parties, etc. all because of 'pregnancy complications,' I would have no life. Pregnancy stress was just a fact of life for me. I had to go to the wedding.

It was a strange wedding for me. The day was beautiful and perfect, but my mind was always floating above all of the conversations. I timidly drank tiny bits of champagne here and there, unsure if I was even pregnant anymore or in the middle of a miscarriage. My stomach was constantly cramping and I'd been bleeding some too. The pain meds helped ease some of the physical discomfort, but my mental state was another matter. I wondered and worried what was going on in my body. As the weekend progressed, I slowly felt better. By the time we got back home, I was desperate for another ultrasound to see what was going on.

We managed to make it back from Kansas City without any emergency hospital visits. My cramps were still there, but not nearly as severe as they had been. About a week later, my RE's office finally got me in for an ultrasound. I was just shy of six weeks pregnant and eager for answers.

Surprisingly, I did not have an ectopic pregnancy. I did, however, *have twins*. The ultrasound technician saw two tiny gestational sacs. I was amazed I was still pregnant. Not only was I still pregnant, but there were *two* babies inside me. I wondered if my prayers had really been answered and if those two little miracles would be God's way of saying he was sorry for my first two losses and he was making it up to me. I couldn't believe it.

I wanted to jump for joy, but after two miscarriages in a row, celebrating wasn't an option. More importantly, one baby was measuring well over a week smaller than the other, so it was possible that one wouldn't make it.

While I wanted to be happy and rejoice in the possibilities, the anxiety of having two little lives in my body filled me with dread. My first thought was that it was going to hurt so much more when I lost them. That was my mindset after I had suffered two miscarriages. I always feared the worst. Things never turned out well for me. Why would that pregnancy have been any different? I wondered *when* I would lose them, rather than *if*. Regardless of my perseverance for continuing to try and conceive, I was still convinced it would end badly.

To make matters worse, my younger sister Abby was pregnant too. Our due dates were only a week apart. I knew that my whole family was extra nervous at that time. Not only did they all fear that I would miscarry again, but they feared the fact that if I did miscarry, I would have to see a niece or nephew of the exact age that my twin babies should have been, for the rest of my life. It added more pressure to the whole pregnancy.

I went through the motions, dutifully going back for our weekly ultrasounds just like we had with our two previous pregnancies. I continued two daily Lovenox injections in my belly and one Progesterone injection in my rear every single day. I was a human pin cushion. Our immediate families both knew about our pregnancy right away too. Taking meds like that was difficult to hide and we lost the option of surprising people with happy pregnancy news a long time ago. Kevin and I both decided that if something ever went wrong with our pregnancy, we'd want our family's support to help us get through it, so there was no point in keeping it a secret.

Remarkably, the smaller baby caught up with the other one and they were both growing in sync with each other and measuring right on track. Of course, that was no comfort to me, I was still a basket-case awaiting that dreaded twelve-week mark to come and ruin everything.

And sure enough, it did.

I was eleven weeks pregnant and we had graduated from our RE and had been seeing a Maternal Fetal Medicine specialist, an OB for high-risk pregnancies. It had been two weeks since my previous ultrasound and both babies looked great. I said my silent prayer as I sat on the edge of the exam table and put my feet in the stirrups.

The ultrasound tech was a short, slightly older woman with long red hair. I could tell something was wrong as soon as she put the wand in. Baby A looked a great deal smaller than Baby B. They label them Baby A and Baby B based on their position in the uterus, whichever baby was closest to the cervix.

I looked over at Kevin as a familiar panic set in. He looked none-the-wiser. He was just ready and excited to see our two babies that we'd already grown so attached to. The tech looked to be avoiding Baby A and was measuring everything else she could when I finally couldn't take it anymore.

"Is Baby A okay?" I asked her hesitantly. She looked uncomfortable and said she was coming to that. I was straining my eyes to see any flicker of life in our little twin. I was searching mostly for the flickering spot in the chest that would indicate a beating heart. I saw nothing.

She finally moved the wand over top of Baby A and ran a measurement. I saw on the screen the baby measured nine weeks in size. I was eleven weeks along. Two weeks prior, the baby measured at nine weeks, which meant there had been no growth in the past two weeks. That wasn't normal. I looked at the tech knowingly and said, "That's not good, is it?"

She gave me an awkward look and continued to peer down at her screen. "We'll look a little closer."

Kevin looked at me confused and said, "What? What is it? What's wrong?"

I snapped angrily back at him and said, "The baby is measuring two weeks small, Kevin. That's not right. It's not good!"

I looked accusingly at the tech as my eyes filled with tears. "There's no heartbeat, is there?"

"Not that I can see," she stated softly.

Then I lost it. I loudly threw out the F-bomb, right in front of the ultrasound tech. I didn't care. I couldn't care. My world crumbled around me once again. Frick, frick, frick, frick, FUCK! This nightmare would never end. I couldn't keep them. They just kept dying on me! That twin was different because it died inside me and I hadn't even known. I hadn't bled or spotted and everything seemed fine. I was bawling at that point. My stomach shook and caused the images on the ultrasound probe to contract with each sob. Our healthy Baby B was wiggling on the screen, but the tears overflowing in my eyes clouded my view.

Kevin looked pleadingly at the tech and said, "So that's it? Is it really gone?"

The tech looked over apologetically and said, "I can't say for sure, we'll have to wait for the doctor."

She pulled the probe out and gently replaced it in its holder. Before she walked out of the room, she handed me a box of tissues. With that, *I knew.* That was all the confirmation I needed. Baby A was gone.

As the door closed behind her, I unleashed on Kevin. "I can't fricken' believe this. I just don't know what I keep doing wrong! Why does this keep happening to us? Fuck!" I screeched. I wanted *both* twins. I felt I deserved them. They were mine—OURS! They were our family. I could have had those babies and been done forever and have wanted for nothing. I thought they were God's answer to our prayers. I couldn't figure out why it kept happening.

Kevin looked despondent. He tried to remind me that Baby B was still okay in there and that we had to stay strong for Baby B. Suddenly, my heart broke all over again, this time for Baby B. Deep down, I knew it was only a matter of time before Baby B died as well.

The doctor looked so sad and sorry when he came in. I knew all hope was gone. He told us these things happen sometimes and that we would continue on with Baby B and things would likely be okay.

When I got home, I was inconsolable. I stripped down to my underwear and bra and crawled into the covers. I relished the feel of the soft sheets against my skin. I was used to this routine. *Amy killed another baby, so it's time to strip down and crawl under the sheets.* It was the same old song and dance.

Losing Baby A proved nothing had changed despite the new meds and acupuncture. Bad things would just keep happening to us. I cried for the loss of Baby A. I cried for the lack of hope I had for Baby B. It was impossible to believe that Baby B would make it. Hell, I had lost three babies in a row. Medically, I knew the odds only got worse after so many consecutive miscarriages. It was just a matter of time. *Poor Baby B.*

The next few weeks, we stayed home every weekend. We only left to go to work and home again. I miraculously passed the dreaded twelve-week milestone and walked on eggshells everywhere I went. I continued my acupuncture and went to weekly ultrasound appointments. I found myself dissecting every cramp and wondering when the end would come. I constantly wondered if the cramps were from my anxiety or if something was really wrong. We used my Doppler frequently, but that only helped for a short time because I knew how quickly things could change. My history had me in a continual state of fear.

I had some mild bleeding episodes then as well. We rushed in, panicking that the bleeding was a sign of another imminent miscarriage. The doctor told us that some bleeding was to be expected with a vanishing twin. We had to see little Baby A at every ultrasound. For the first few weeks, they still had to take images of our lost twin to ensure it wasn't growing or anything out of the ordinary since their initial diagnosis. The ultrasound techs would always warn me. They'd look at me apologetically and say, "I'm sorry, but we have to take images of the other one too." It was fine though. I could see it anyway. In the ultrasound shots they sent us home with, we could see our lost baby's gestational sac and shape. Those poor, poor babies. Their lot in life was to be stuck with me for a few short weeks and die. It was only a matter of time before my body aborted them. When would it end for this one?

When I hit fourteen weeks we were just a couple of days away from having another ultrasound. It was a quiet Saturday night. My sister and her husband came over. Our conversations were just starting to veer toward the possibility of this baby making it, but I hadn't felt well all night. I was cramping slightly and anxious to go to bed because I wouldn't have to worry for a few hours. My body and mind would get a break.

My body never got that break. I awoke in the middle of the night to red blood all over my pants and sheets.

"Kevin, wake up! There's blood everywhere!" I yelled.

Kevin shot out of bed and helped rush me into the bathroom. Poor Kevin! How many times had I awakened him out of a deep, mindless slumber, crying about blood or cramps? How would he ever sleep peacefully again for the rest of his life?

I sat down and filled the toilet with bloody clots. "Go get the Doppler!" I said urgently and wiped myself as clean as I could manage.

Once again, I laid my bloody body on the bathroom floor next to my bloody pants and checked the baby's heart rate. It was still there. The heartbeat was 150 beats per minute, which was relatively normal but that moment felt like the worst kind of deja vu.

Kevin and I hurried to the ER. I continued to pass clots and blood. Upon examination, the ER doctor told me my cervix was, once again, wide open.

I was just shocked at this point and confused with why this kept happening in this same manner. My cramps were intense and came in waves. I could tell the doctor was certain the baby wasn't alive, but I knew better.

They did an ultrasound and as I expected, Baby B was still there and alive, measuring four days ahead with a good, healthy heart rate. Even in the midst of the horrible reoccurring nightmare, I couldn't help but feel proud of my little peanut for measuring ahead and already showing mommy signs of overachievement.

The emergency room doctor informed us that I would be sent up to labor and delivery because the OB/GYN on call happened to be my Reproductive Endocrinologist. The same RE who helped me get pregnant in the first place. I was hopeful he could help keep Baby B inside me since he knew my history so well.

I was sitting in the hospital bed with the rails up as they pushed me out the door. I suddenly felt a sharp popping sensation from inside my lower belly. I concurrently felt gushing liquid between my legs. It felt like a ball of pressure had been released inside of me.

"I just felt a popping sensation! What does that mean?" I asked worriedly.

"I'm not sure, but we just need to get you upstairs and have the OB/GYN take a look at you," said the nurse as she pushed my bed upstairs.

By the time they got me upstairs, I was desperate to use the restroom and clean myself up. Whenever I went into an emergency room, they always made me take all of my clothes off and get into a gown. They would typically lay a blue pad below me, to catch all that was coming out. I was forced to lie there in all my bloody discharge while the medical staff came in and out to check on me.

I was full of bloody stuff down there and needed to simply sit on a toilet and wipe myself clean. While we waited for my RE, a nurse came in and introduced herself as Amy. Easy name to remember since it was also mine.

"Do you think I'm okay to get up and go to the restroom? I really want to wipe down there," I asked.

"I'm sure that will be just fine, do you need help to the bathroom?" she inquired as she typed into the computer.

"No, I can manage," I replied as I looked over at Kevin getting all our stuff situated on the pull out couch in the room.

As I sat down on the toilet and wiped, I felt something hanging between my legs. A feeling of dread washed over my whole body.

"Nurse Amy!" I shouted, "There's something hanging out of me!" I cried.

I gasped for breath while I held *whatever it was* in place. Nurse Amy rushed in and grabbed a tall, clear beaker located inside the cupboard opposite the sink. She quickly put on some surgical gloves and reached in between my legs.

I finally looked down. Nestled inside her two bloodied white gloves was my baby, limp and completely lifeless. She placed it gently in the beaker and came back to help clean me up. My eyes were wide and welling with tears. I stared, horrified at the bloody mass of a baby crumpled inside the beaker. I panted out three large breaths and bawled. Hard. *Did that really just happen? Did I really just have a baby pulled out of my vagina over a toilet bowl in a hospital?*

She looked at me sadly, knowing she didn't have to tell me what just happened. This one was so much more obvious than the others, because it was a couple of weeks older. At fourteen weeks old, I could clearly see the baby's head, about the size of a golf ball. It had long skinny arms and legs, a belly, hips—everything. A perfectly formed baby, ruined, by *my* stupid body. I wondered why I couldn't keep them in, and how I kept ruining our babies lives. The tiny form was small, much too small. But perfect.

Kevin walked in and took a look at the beaker on the counter. I saw a sick feeling roll over his expression. He didn't need help figuring this one out. He knew. I had delivered our baby over a toilet, into a beaker.

He remained frozen in place while I continued to sob into my blood stained hands on the toilet.

Nurse Amy's voice cut into the heated scene, "Dad, can you help Mom out here?"

Kevin snapped back to attention, his far away thoughts were brought back to the situation at hand. He came over and knelt beside me, rubbed my back and said soothing things, like *it'll be okay. We're okay.*

The irony of that moment was that for the very first time, someone referred to Kevin and me as Mom and Dad. *Jesus, my cup really runneth over now.*

I couldn't shout expletives or lash out at Kevin like usual. I didn't have the energy. I just continued crying on the toilet bowl. I had just delivered our second twin into my very own hands over a hospital toilet. *Four babies gone now.* What could be said for such an awful scene?

When I'd finally pulled myself together enough to hobble back to the hospital bed, I felt my emotions evaporate. I was empty and alone. I had no baby to worry about and nothing to live for. There was nothing to survive for. I was ripped and bloodied and didn't give a crap anymore.

The RE came in and examined me. He looked sad and misplaced. He knew this was the fourth baby we'd lost and he had no words to ease our pain. He looked scared. In the background I heard him tell Kevin that we needed to do a D&C right away because I was still hemorrhaging blood. Before I knew it, they were wheeling me off to surgery. Again. Three D&Cs. *Four dead babies.* This was my life.

When I woke up from surgery, I felt hollow. Vacant. Despite my pessimism, the fourteen-week-old baby had burrowed a hole into my heart, and I had dared to hope, even though reality should have taught me better. We made it past the elusive twelve-week mark that seemed to be our kryptonite, but it didn't matter.

Nurse Amy came in and said that the baby was in the *Quiet Room* and inquired if we would like to see it. I looked at Kevin and said, "This might be the only baby of ours we ever see."

Kevin looked at me and I could tell he would do whatever I wanted at that point. He was tired of seeing me hurt and bleeding. He would have walked through fire just to give me some sense of peace.

The nurse brought the baby in wrapped in a knitted hooded blanket that was way too big for it. Sad, yet beautiful. Everything was formed. Ten fingers, ten toes, a nose, a mouth, and little eyelid slits. The skin was pretty translucent and was a sort of bluish tan color with veins.

I looked closely and thought it looked like Kevin. The nurse told me she thought it was a boy because if you looked down at its private area, you could definitely see something hanging there. Testing later told us it was another healthy girl. The clitoris develops first and that's what we were seeing that day. Everything was just so tiny. Microscopic, but still perfectly formed.

Amy said Baby A had come out with Baby B and it was amazing how differently they looked. We chose not to see Baby A. We knew there wouldn't be much to look at since it had been gone for so long. We just looked at Baby B and prepared our goodbyes. Tears were forming in my eyes so quickly. My vision blurred as I knew I needed to say something to this baby.

"I'm sorry baby. I wish things could have been different. I wish I could have kept you inside of me the whole time. I wish you would have come out squirmy and pink with chubby cheeks. But we just can't do it. I don't know why, we just can't."

Kevin sat next to me on the bed as we held our child. He was at a loss for words. Words don't come easily to most men in emotionally charged situations. I knew he never blamed me for any of it and he would never let me say it was my fault, but that's what I was thinking. I chose to think it silently because there was no need arguing about *the facts*.

The nurse eventually came in and took the baby. Kevin and I both continued to lie together on the small hospital bed. I asked him to hold me tighter and he did. We cried as time passed by.

A while later my RE came in to talk to me. I could

tell he had no idea what to say. It was obvious he had been on the verge of losing hope for me. For him to see a patient constantly make it past the first trimester and suddenly abort the baby is not common. The words adoption and surrogacy were thrown around. In that moment, I was ready for that. I'd been pregnant a total of thirty-eight weeks and had no baby to show for it. It had been a tough couple years of miscarriages.

Before we left the hospital, Nurse Amy came in with grief pamphlets. One was called "The Story of the Dragonfly." It was actually a pretty neat story, drawing a parallel between what happens when people go to heaven and what happens to dragonflies when they grow their wings. Apparently, dragonflies start their lives as water bugs and eventually mature and develop enough to leave the water. Unfortunately, they can never go back into the water after that, which leaves their dragonfly friends sad and distraught. The Story of the Dragonfly goes on to explain that even if they could go back into the water, they wouldn't want to because the world above the water was so beautiful and wondrous that they shouldn't feel sad or miss them. So we should take comfort in knowing that when our loved ones move on to heaven.

Nurse Amy also gave me four tiny gold rings, each packaged in individual clear plastic bags. When she handed them to me she explained that she had seen in my chart that I had miscarried before. She assumed we never received the gold rings because it was only something

Labor and Delivery handed out, so she hoped it was okay that she gave me four today, instead of two. That broke my heart. She cared enough to take the extra step and look a little deeper. She casually told me she'd seen some women wear them around their necks as memorials. She had no idea she had given me a gift I would wear every day. In that moment, I knew I would never forget Nurse Amy.

One thing I learned was that miscarrying in Labor and Delivery was a lot better than miscarrying in the emergency room. The ER never sent me home with grief pamphlets or gold rings as memorials. They just checked me out and sent me home, empty and alone.

11: RESEARCH

> *Nancy, Amy's Mom*
> *It was easy to think of this road as Amy's journey. She was relentless in her medical research and studied to figure out why it was happening to her. While I admired my daughter for being her own advocate in finding a way to have a successful pregnancy, I also wondered how many times Kevin could pick her up off the bathroom floor? Would she bleed out on the way to the ER? I knew there were medical personnel that would take care of Amy, but who took care of Kevin? When my phone would ring in the night, I would take a deep breath before answering because I feared it was another loss for them. If it was Kevin calling, I was really scared. If it was Amy, at least I knew she was alive. I wanted it so badly for them. There was little I could do except sit on the sidelines and wait. It became a custom that while I couldn't do anything to make it happen, I could help pick up the pieces. I would drive two hours and get there as soon as I could to hug and cry with her. I did laundry, got groceries, and made a few meals, specifically the family favorite comfort food—Cheesy Potato Soup. These things were always done in that order because that's what this Mom could do. Each time as I headed home from those trips, I would pray that the next time I was out there in this role, it would be to help her bring home a new baby. We were a family of believers and I had faith it would happen but I still worried Amy would lose her faith on this journey.*

December twelfth was when I lost my fourteen-week-old angel baby and the holidays were coming up. I had another follow up with my OB/GYN. She graciously prescribed me Xanax, Zoloft and Percocet for anxiety, depression and pain. Boy, I must have looked like a hot mess in her office for her to give me a cocktail like that! Needless to say, I was prepared to live the holidays in a numb fog. Anything that would blur the image of my pregnant younger sister was what I wanted on tap.

I'd hardly been home a day and really hadn't properly grieved. My brain kicked into overdrive and I decided I wasn't done yet. It was amazing what I'd put myself through when I wanted something bad enough. I had such a visceral need to carry my own child. It didn't matter how bruised, bloodied and broken I was. Nothing could top having a baby.

I was consumed with researching online to find answers for why I kept miscarrying right after the first trimester. It didn't matter where I was, I was online searching. I emailed the public library to request specific medical textbooks pertaining to my issues. I did so much research that I was eventually able to understand the majority of those books.

Surrogacy was an option that my RE had seriously thrown out at me. I researched it and discovered it wasn't the easy solution everyone thought it was. It would allow Kevin and me to have our own genetic child by permitting his sperm and my egg to be fertilized in a petri dish. Then it would be transferred into someone else, but that wasn't all. First of all, we'd have to find someone who would carry the child for me. Each state had different laws regarding surrogacy. In some states, surrogates can receive financial compensation, but in other states, they can't. In some states a surrogate has to have had one child of her own before acting as a surrogate, in other states they don't. Surrogacy is a very difficult minefield to navigate. To get that perfect embryo, it would require Kevin, me, and our surrogate to do in-vitro fertilization. It would cost an easy fifteen grand our insurance would not cover. Not cheap. And that didn't eliminate all the risk of miscarriage.

I did consider asking my older sister, Amber, to be our surrogate. She had had two boys at that point and I knew she didn't want any more children. Her pregnancies were all blissfully uneventful and she knew what being pregnant involved. However, getting our insurance to cover her would be a major ordeal. Her health insurance wouldn't cover anything pregnancy related if they knew she was carrying someone else's child. To hide that from her insurance would have been insurance fraud. There was no way we were going to do something like that. Plus, there were legal sides to surrogacy once the baby was born. We'd have to hire a lawyer to draw up paperwork in order to actually adopt our own baby.

In the end I never officially asked her, which was good because I don't think it was something she would have been particularly interested in helping with. She wasn't someone who enjoyed pregnancy, and to ask someone to give up nine months of their life was a lot.

The most frustrating part about surrogacy was the ignorance of the general public. If they heard someone had issues with recurrent pregnancy loss, they suggested surrogacy in random conversation. It was ludicrous. They hadn't the slightest clue what it took. Not to mention, they seemed to assume we hadn't already considered that option.

Overall, it was a dark time for me and Kevin. He was angry with me about always being online and wanting to put myself through it all again. He wanted me to get off the computer and talk to *him*. I didn't want to talk to him because I felt he wasn't on my level of understanding. At times I even resented him for that. I felt like I devoted a lot more into having a baby than he had because I was putting in the time and research while he just sat back and watched me make all the decisions pertaining to meds, appointments, doctors, etc.

Mostly, Kevin wanted to talk about adoption. For him, it seemed like the easiest answer with more of a guarantee. With adoption there was no risk to my health and we didn't have to suffer through nine months of agony waiting for things to fall apart as they always had. I knew he couldn't stomach the thought of watching me go through another loss. But I felt adoption would be like a consolation prize at that point. It felt like quitting. I didn't want to be forced in to adoption and I wasn't ready to consider alternatives. I sure as hell wasn't willing to go through all that hell and receive no answers. I could fix this! I had to fix this! If I persevered, we would figure it out and get our own genetically-connected child. Adoption just wasn't something I was ready to contemplate, especially because the cost of adoption was upwards towards thirty-thousand dollars! That was definitely more than the medical treatment I was seeking.

I understood why he wanted to adopt. He loved me so much and he had to repeatedly watch me in physical and emotional agony. It was becoming normal for Kevin to watch me bleed all over our bathroom, knowing there was nothing he could do. He wasn't Jesus or a medically trained professional. He was just Kevin, my husband. He was the one who had to pick up the pieces every time they fell, which so far, had been every time.

However, understanding his point of view didn't change the fact that it was my body. I was willing to put my body through *anything* if it meant I would conceive and carry my own child. I could look at my sister's two boys and see a resemblance. I had people tell me that my sister's oldest son looked more like me than her. That thrilled me. I loved feeling that genetic link to him, knowing people could mistake me for being his mom. I wanted to be a mom so badly that my attachment to my sister's kids grew stronger. They were the closest thing I had to being a mother.

Since I was only twenty-seven years old and still in the prime reproductive years, I was determined to exhaust all of my options. Fertility issues and probability of miscarriage would only get worse the older I got. I knew I could adopt at any age.

Through all my research online, I found a recurrent pregnancy loss specialist in Chicago. Her name was Dr. Patel and she was originally from Canada. She was the only doctor I found in the United States who specialized in recurrent pregnancy loss, so I was thankful that she was located in the Midwest. It was still a nine-hour drive from our home in Sioux Falls, SD, but it was drivable. I researched a couple of other doctors in New York and Las Vegas and was interested in some of the newer research they were working on, but was unsure how feasible doctoring with somebody that far away would be. Remote doctoring wasn't covered by my insurance either. I had to physically see the doctor in order to get my insurance to cover the testing. Chicago didn't sound too bad at all. I was just grateful that there might be someone out there who could give us some answers.

Although Kevin and I weren't seeing eye-to-eye, he agreed to go to Chicago to have more diagnostic testing done. Kevin strongly felt that if we didn't get any answers, we shouldn't try again. I, however, was in the mindset that I would kill myself before I gave up. I wasn't sure if those were suicidal thoughts or simply thoughts of desperation, but I refused to put myself first. I refused to believe that my babies' lives would be lost in vain. I refused to accept the journey was at its end. I couldn't let it go until I knew what was causing my babies to die.

Before all that, the Reproductive Endocrinologist made an appointment for us with the hospital psychologist. He didn't really give us a choice. He put it down in his notes like it was something we had to do. That told me how horrible I must have looked the week following my loss. He was the RE that witnessed the loss. He knew me well by now. The nurses I had been close with throughout my struggles told me that my RE had walked around the office horribly depressed after my last loss happened. I was somewhat surprised that he was just as human as I was. I had previously put doctors on a pedestal and thought they witnessed traumas like mine without being affected. To hear my tragedy had personally affected him had warmed my heart a little. But to know my *doctor* was depressed about my situation only made me more terrified. If a trained medical specialist was scared and hopeless, what could the future possibly hold for me?

***

Amy Daws

12: COUNSELING

Kristen, Amy's Friend

When I found out I was going to lose my first son, Amy was one of the first people to offer her support. I had the image of us sitting on either end of my couch, talking deeply about the love we felt for our lost babies and the unending heartbreak we would forever endure. Though she may not have known it, she helped me more than she knew that day. Through her losses, she had found more strength than she maybe even realized. She gave me advice, explained to me how I might feel and let me grieve. It was that type of "counseling" that helped get me through some of my darkest days. And in some ways, I'm thankful—because I made such a wonderful friend.

Closing in on thirty-five weeks pregnant, the baby's nursery was top priority. My C-section date was less than three weeks away and I needed her nursery to be special. It needed to be homemade and from the heart.

I walked into the small nursery, holding a wall decal that needed to go up. "Kevin, I need your help hanging this please," I shouted toward the door as I thoughtfully looked at the wall and tried to determine if I wanted it centered on the wall or centered over the crib.

The crib and dresser were a light blonde wood and hand-me-downs from my older sister. They had two boys and were done having kids. That gift saved us a bundle on the cost of the baby's room.

Kevin walked into the room noisily, swishing in his windbreaker pants and t-shirt. "Oh, you want to hang this now?" he asked as he scratched his head.

"Yeah, we need to get this room done. It's so close, I just want it finished and off my mind," I said as I held up the decal on the center of the wall. "Does this look good in the center?"

"Sure, whatever you think, babe. You're better at this stuff than I am," Kevin said as he supported the decal on the wall so I could step back and take a look. "Are you sure we have time to do this? Don't you have that support group to go to soon?" he asked.

"Yes, but we have time. It can't take longer than thirty minutes. I don't need to leave until then, so let's just get this up already," I said frustrated that he was trying to procrastinate—like always.

We did need to hurry though. I was always late to my

support group. We met every other week. It was a small group of four women and a counselor. All of us had multiple miscarriages, but nobody had as many as me. Leave it to me to stand out in a crowd in the most pathetic way possible.

As Kevin and I peeled back the batting, we revealed the scripty black font quote that was to be the perfect focal point to the nursery:

If the road to get here would have been easy, we wouldn't have you.

My friend Ashley helped me come up with it. I knew I wanted to put something special on the wall that depicted our journey without writing the obvious: *We lost five babies before we had you.* Ashley was always so good with words. I would go through old emails and read incredibly inspiring advice and words of wisdom she had given me through all our struggles. She's that friend that always answered her phone. Despite the fact that she was not even remotely thinking about having babies of her own yet, she still always found a way to relate. I felt like her heart broke just as much as mine every time I called her to tell her we had lost another one. I needed a friend like that who would cry with me.

"It looks good, right?" I asked Kevin wanting to revel in the moment a bit.

Kevin came up behind me and laced his hands through mine and said, "It looks really good babe. I think it's awesome."

It did look awesome. The black script letters stuck to the wall revealing a faint orange peel texture through them. I had ordered the saying online from one of those decorating websites that specialized in custom wall sayings for the home.

"The whole room is awesome. Grandma's mobile over the crib, Mom's quilt, it all came together and it's all homemade. I hope this baby can feel the love in this room," I said as I felt anxiety rising in my chest again. I really needed to bring a baby home to this room or I would really lose it.

The mobile my Grandma made was my other favorite part of the room. It was a variety of different sized crocheted balls that hung at different levels from fishing line so they appeared to be floating above the crib. The colors in the room weren't the typical baby colors either. They were a vibrant fuchsia, lime green, reds, blacks and greys. This was a room our little girl could grow up in; still thinking it was cool into her school years. I was never one to like pastels or frilly baby things.

We also had her name hanging above her closet in

adorable customized wooden letters. One of my online Mommy friends I met through an infertility board contacted me and asked if she could make the baby's name with wooden letters as a gift to me. *Everybody was rooting for us.*

We had planned on naming our daughter Lorelei. Pronounced lor-a-lie. I never referred to her in my belly that way. That would be too cocky. The Gods would surely strike me down dead if I were that presumptuous.

Lorelei was a name of two characters on my all time favorite TV show, *Gilmore Girls.* It was a show about a single Mom named Lorelei who was raising her teenage daughter on her own. Her daughter's name was also Lorelei but everyone called her Rory. The name Lorelei was perfect. It was a classic name, yet not something heard very often. The two Lorelei's on the show were funny, smart, and witty. They valued books, music, and educating themselves. Everything I would ever want in my daughter. I couldn't wait to introduce the show to my daughter as she grew up. *There I went, making assumptions.*

I sat down in the new overstuffed rocker/recliner and looked around the room, relishing it all.

"You feeling okay, babe?" Kevin asked as he watched me rub my taut belly.

"Yeah, I'm good. I just want to sit here a minute and enjoy it all," I said as I extended the foot of the recliner.

Kevin kissed me sweetly on the lips and left the room. I looked around the room and felt overwhelmed by emotions. I rubbed my belly and let out a slow breath.

Please baby, pleeeeease stay in there and stay alive. I need you to make it. I need you to hang in there. We're so close. If I lose you now, it will kill me. Seriously, I won't make it without you, little one. You and I are a packaged deal now. We've come too far together. I want you here so, so bad. My heart hurts thinking about it. The closer we get, the more anxious I feel, so please don't do anything crazy. Just keep growing and thriving in there and I'll do my best to get you out safely, okay? My tears fell freely down my cheeks and onto my neck and chest.

For the past month I begged my doctor to take our baby early because I was convinced something bad would happen. Gestationally, I was far enough along for her to survive outside of the womb. She may need to stay in the neonatal intensive care unit for a little while, but she would live. He would just smile politely at me and tell me to hang in there. *Thanks a lot, doc.*

I pushed the foot of the recliner down and left the nursery, knowing I was going to be late, once again, for my support group.

I pulled into the parking lot and made my way into the hospital clinic. The support group was officially affiliated through the hospital I miscarried all my babies in, but we weren't allowed to mention any specific doctors' names when we were sharing various stories. I imagine it was a liability issue and they didn't want the groups to turn into doctor bashing. The point was emotional support, not medical advice or experiences.

The first group I joined was a group of mothers who had second trimester losses. My friend, Kristen, asked me if I would come with her. She had been attending since the loss of her son. Technically my losses occurred in the second trimester, so I agreed.

Three of my five losses occurred at or after twelve weeks. The small issue with this group was that all of those women had only suffered one loss. Many of them named their babies and had funeral services. Choosing to never name any of my losses was a personal thing. I never really felt like I had the opportunity with my first two losses because those occurred in the emergency room and the ER doesn't really give you any guidance on how to deal with a loss. Then after my fourteen-weeks-along twin loss, where we got to hold the baby, I just couldn't bring myself to name it or hold any type of funeral service. I never did that with my first two losses, so it didn't seem fair. I wanted to treat each of my angel babies equally. I feared that if I did something different for my third miscarriage, perhaps the baby would end up in a different place than the others. I wanted them all together. I didn't know if those thoughts made any sense but it was how I felt. I always left the disposal of the babies up to the hospital. I never asked too many questions about how they disposed of the babies. I guess I didn't want to know the details. I wanted to envision them as beautiful spirits all together that moved on to heaven.

When I met mothers who had named their deceased babies, taken pictures of them and memorialized them, I felt uncomfortable. I spoke with the counselor and she agreed that this group was not the right fit for me and she had another group of moms that had multiple miscarriages. This group seemed like a slightly better fit, but still not perfect because all those women had losses in early pregnancy. So, once again, I was standing out in a crowd and not quite fitting into a specific *box*, so to speak.

I walked into the small conference room and the four ladies and counselor were all sitting in wheelie office chairs around a large boardroom style table. "Hey guys, sorry I'm late again."

They all gave me big smiles. When I conceived Lorelei, I had a heart to heart with the counselor, Margie, to decide if I would still be welcome in the group. I was barely five weeks pregnant, but I knew how hard it was to be around other pregnant women while so desperately wanting a baby. The last thing I wanted to do was flaunt a pregnancy in front of my grieving friends. Margie said she would speak to the group and let me know. They all welcomed me with open arms. From experience, I discovered it was easier to welcome a pregnancy from a woman who had a tough go of it, especially if they still didn't have a child at home. If they had a child at home and were suffering secondary infertility or secondary recurrent pregnancy loss, it was still a shame, but at least they had a child to love every night and their dreams of becoming a parent had already come true.

As I made my way around the table I noticed all of their eyes glancing eagerly at my belly. That's something I would never get used to. When I was noticeably pregnant, people rarely ever looked at my face; they eyeballed my belly instead. It was odd to have people stare at my body unabashedly.

"How are you feeling?" asked Katy, the thirty-seven year old Mom who had three miscarriages in a row between five and seven weeks pregnant.

"Oh, I'm feeling okay I guess," I laughed awkwardly as I sat down in the chair next to her. "Thirty-five weeks and counting." *Don't sound too confident Amy, don't sound too confident!*

Margie looked at me expectantly. "And you've got your C-section scheduled for when again?"

"May ninth," I said looking around at everybody and nodding.

"Oh man, that's coming up so fast, I can't believe you started this group when you were newly pregnant," said Rachael, another mom who had lost two in a row, one at ten weeks and another at eight.

"I know," I sighed. "I always wondered if it would be weird for me to stay in this group if I was currently pregnant, but I don't know what I'd do without you guys to come to every couple of months and vent."

Katy turned her chair towards me. "We had to see you through this whole pregnancy, Amy. I feel just as anxious as you, but I can't imagine not being there for you through it all."

I smiled kindly at her. For me, this group was a place to vent my feelings of fear of losing this baby. Most of us followed each other through roads of diagnostic procedures and tests. I had been through most of the tests, so I was able to offer a lot of advice on what they should expect or whom they could talk to next. None of their stories were like mine. None of them reached that magical twelve-week mark, but they had been through tough times all the same.

"Do you still talk to that doctor in Chicago? The one who placed your cerclage?" Gina asked. Gina had a seven-year-old boy at home, but she and her husband had been having difficulty conceiving their second child for several years.

"I email him a lot. I'm always asking him questions and he's so good at alleviating my fears. Seriously, he's the best doctor. I've never met a doctor who actually encouraged me to email him. He even calls me on my cell phone, just to check in," I shook my head incredulously.

Margie smiled warmly at me and said, "Shall we begin?" We all settled in to listen to a poem she found online. I looked around at all the women and thought back to Chicago and how truly far we'd come since then. I was nearing the home stretch of the pregnancy, but I still wasn't convinced that I wouldn't be telling a story of a new heartache.

***

Amy Daws

13: CHICAGO

Kevin, Amy's Husband

I remember Chicago as the city that gave us Dr. Haney. He was the doctor that gave us another shot at having our own child. I have so much respect for him. I remember during Amy's pregnancy and after the surgery, she would email him at least once a week with a question. What amazed me was that even with all his patients and all his other responsibilities, he always emailed Amy back. He always gave very detailed replies, rather than a simple yes or no. He was confident things would work out for us, which made him a great source of hope for us.

Kevin and I were on our third road trip back to Chicago in the last six months. We'd been seeing the Canadian recurrent pregnancy loss specialist and we were exhausted and disappointed with the progress so far. Every trip we made to Chicago, we expected to get some big news pertaining to the results of all of the tests I'd undergone. Up until then, it consisted of a lot of talking about our history, explaining in specific and graphic detail every loss and symptom that led up to it. There was a lot of chart copying and waiting to get stuff transferred from the hospital in our hometown. They took tons of blood. One time they took twenty-five vials of blood in one sitting. I asked the lab technician if it was the most vials they had ever taken from one person. She said maybe one or two vials shy of the most. If I was reaching record status at a huge university metropolitan hospital, I must have really been screwed up.

After waiting nearly two hours in the waiting room amongst a number of pregnant women, we finally got called back to see Dr. Patel. She was a short, stocky woman with medium-length brown hair. She had a slight Canadian accent and was very short and curt in our conversations. "Well, your uterine wall and lining looked good from the uterine scope we did the last time you were here. The only thing I noted during the procedure was that the camera passed through your cervix easily, like butter. Typically, a lot of force is required to push the camera through the cervix, so I think you may have some cervical issues and I recommend an empirical vaginal cerclage to be placed around twelve weeks upon your next pregnancy.

Well, this was new. Kevin and I looked at her, dumbfounded that we'd finally got some new information.

"Also, we have confirmed the results of your clotting disorder and you have what's called, Antiphospholipid Antibody Syndrome, specifically a strain called Lupus Anticoagulant. It's only active when you are pregnant, so, upon your next pregnancy, we would want you on Lovenox blood thinners twice a day. This is a therapeutic dose to treat that clotting issue. So that means you'll have to do injections twice a day. Okay?" She looked at us very matter of fact.

I looked back at her and crinkled my brow. We had been on Lovenox during the twin pregnancy, so this wasn't a new approach. With my history of a clot, it was the standard of care. Not to mention, I had known from previous experience that doctors would prescribe empirical blood thinners to help with unexplained recurrent pregnancy loss because blood thinners had proven to be an off label aide in preventing miscarriage. By prescribing Lovenox, they were attempting an 'everything-but-the-kitchen-sink approach.'

I cleared my throat. "We've already tried blood thinners."

She looked back at me and stated rather abruptly, "Yes, but your local maternal fetal medicine specialist reduced your dose and I don't agree with that. I want your anticoagulation therapy to be followed by a hematologist, not an MFM."

I wasn't satisfied on the blood thinner recommendation but the cervical issue was something I had suspected before. I had been very busy researching on a website called *Abbyloopers.org* for quite some time. I even chatted with the site administrators and had already gathered a lot of information. My losses weren't traditional to most women diagnosed with an IC, which is short for incompetent cervix. Most women with IC suffered pregnancy losses between sixteen to twenty weeks. Mine were between twelve and fourteen weeks. However, being diligent in my research and through the very knowledgeable women on the *Abbyloopers* site, I had come across a lot of information on Dr. Arther Haney, who was employed at the same hospital we were being treated at in Chicago. He was a renowned expert on incompetent cervical issues and famous for a procedure called a transabdominal cerclage, more commonly referred to as a TAC. It would be a slightly controversial procedure and was much more invasive than the vaginal cerclage. But it touted a much higher success rate.

"What about doing a transabdominal cerclage instead of a vaginal cerclage like you're suggesting?" I asked hesitantly. "Dr. Haney is a colleague of yours, isn't he?"

She squinted her eyes, scrutinizing my question. "A transabdominal cerclage is far too invasive for what your issues are. First of all, it's permanent and forces you to have a C-section delivery. If you suffer another loss after twelve weeks pregnant, the baby will be too large to pass through the cervical opening because of that band. A C-section is a major surgery, especially if you miscarry and we have to operate on a womb as tiny as twelve weeks. C-sections are designed to cut across tight, taut muscles of a nine-month pregnancy. Not a pregnancy that hasn't reached full term."

"I'm just concerned that waiting until I'm twelve weeks pregnant to place a vaginal cerclage might be too late for me because things could already be going downhill in there," I replied back confidently.

She shook her head at me dismissively. "We can put your vaginal cerclage in at ten weeks if you like."

That effectively ended our discussion and we left Chicago feeling a little confused and perplexed. This wasn't any information we couldn't have received in Sioux Falls. An empirical vaginal cerclage would have probably been the next step my doctor would have tried, so that wasn't anything extraordinary. The lupus anticoagulant clotting disorder required the same treatment protocol we'd already been trying during the twin pregnancy loss. So we felt like we'd wasted a lot of time and money for virtually the same answers.

When we got back to Sioux Falls, I still wasn't satisfied. I had read online that Dr. Haney gave free telephone consultations, so I didn't need to worry about insurance coverage. I figured it wouldn't hurt to at least talk to someone who's an expert in the cervical field.

A few days later, Kevin and I both met at home over our lunch hours for our scheduled phone consultation with Dr. Haney. We sat at the kitchen table, staring at the phone like eager children on Christmas morning, gawking at a pile of presents. We were reaching for a lifeline.

After dealing with a somewhat overly confident recurrent pregnancy loss specialist for the past six months, Dr. Haney was like a breath of fresh air. He started our conversation asking many thoughtful and detailed questions about our history. I described in graphic detail each one of our horrific nightmares. I got emotional several times throughout the discussion and was thankful to have Kevin there to finish my sentences when it got too difficult. I would compose myself and take over the conversation again because I was never satisfied with Kevin's story-telling abilities. Dr. Haney listened patiently through every single story of loss and waited for me to finish each description without interruption.

After commending us on pushing for answers and taking the initiative to call him, he conceded that he thought I had a very early form of incompetent cervix and that a vaginal cerclage would not be the best choice. Since my losses were occurring between twelve to fourteen weeks, it was likely my cervix was already being compromised, beginning to shorten or become unstable, earlier than ten weeks.

He told us that I made an excellent candidate for a pre-pregnancy transabdominal cerclage, or a TAC. The idea of having this surgery done prior to achieving pregnancy was music to my ears. Having any type of procedure done during pregnancy was a scary thought, because my body was never stable during pregnancy. I was to the point where I refused pelvic exams during our multiple trips to the ER. I was worried that too much stimulation in my vaginal area would cause infection or disruption.

Dr. Haney explained how a TAC was different than a vaginal cerclage. The band would be placed at the top of the cervix instead of the bottom. It provided less risk of funneling and bulging membranes. The band would be placed at the top of my cervix to stabilize it, leaving a small opening to allow menstruation and insemination to pass through. We can still get pregnant through normal intercourse or through IUI or IVF if need be. Most importantly, a successfully placed TAC had a ninety-nine percent success rate and typically yielded full term, healthy babies. Many women with simple, less invasive vaginal cerclages ended up on bed rest and delivered prematurely. I didn't want that if I could help it.

Finally, Kevin and I felt like we had something that could be done to help us on our journey. It was a real and tangible thing that was more than just "wait and see." I couldn't get the surgery scheduled fast enough. I knew we would have to fly in because Chicago was a nine-hour car ride and that would not be easy to do after an abdominal surgery.

Amazingly, Kevin's employer offered to give us some American Airline vouchers they had accrued. Kevin came home and told me that his boss pulled him aside and gave them to him. Apparently the company had a board meeting that day and was trying to find somewhere useful for those vouchers to go. It was to the point where Kevin's coworkers and bosses knew when we were pregnant again because suddenly Kevin would have weekly doctor appointments he had to be gone for. He never missed an ultrasound if he could help it because we never knew when the ultrasound would come that would deliver bad news.

Thankfully, his colleagues didn't pressure Kevin into announcing our news. They all feigned ignorance and we appreciated that. Whenever another loss would occur, as they almost always did, Kevin would come clean and tell them we'd been pregnant for a few months and suffered another loss so he would need some time off to grieve and help me heal.

So when his company gave us airline vouchers, it made me emotional. It was like they were giving us permission to continue trying. To continue dreaming! I knew we didn't need their permission; it was our journey, our choice, but at this point we'd had three miscarriages in a row. Undoubtedly, people were starting to have their own opinions, judgments and doubts. I'm sure many couldn't understand why we kept going and didn't pursue adoption or surrogacy because surely that had to be easier than going through loss after loss. But there was so much more to it than that.

A month after our phone consult with Dr. Haney, about the transabdominal cerclage, we flew into Chicago for the surgery. I had called earlier to inform Dr. Patel about our decision to proceed with a TAC. She told me again that she didn't think it was necessary, but it was ultimately our choice. I had hoped that she might pop her head in to say hello during my recovery, but she never did.

The hotel we stayed in the night before my surgery surprised us with an upgraded room. I'd never had an upgraded room in my entire life. I even put in requests to hotels with pleas like, "It's our anniversary and we'd love a complimentary upgrade." And nada. So when we walked into a two-story suite, I was floored. It felt like a sign. Things were finally starting to look up for us.

I couldn't eat anything after 10:00 PM, so Kevin and I walked to a fancy restaurant downtown and grabbed a late dinner. Kevin and I had visited Chicago a few times. It's my favorite city to explore. The city lights and the hustle and bustle of downtown Chicago were exhilarating. The food alone was worth the trip. The restaurant was dark with glitzy decorations and mood lighting. We were seated in a cozy booth against a wall covered in an exquisite mosaic tile design. We went all out and ordered a cheese flight appetizer, two meals and crème brulèe with coffee for dessert. It felt like the night before our wedding all over again. We were giddy and excited because we were doing something major. We were starting another chapter in our lives.

We arrived at the hospital early the next morning. As I changed into the surgical gown and cap, the nurse handed me a pregnancy test and told me I needed to go to the restroom and pee on it. Dr. Haney had warned me beforehand that I'd have to do this because they wouldn't perform the surgery if I were newly pregnant. There was too much risk to do surgery in early pregnancy, so if it came out positive, we would have to reschedule the surgery for a later date when the baby had developed more.

As I peed on the stick I was tortured with what I wanted the outcome to be, which was just ridiculous. We had just flown over the entire state of Iowa to get an amazing surgical procedure done in hopes it would help me stop miscarrying. Nevertheless, I couldn't shake the desire I got every time I peed on a stick to see that positive line turn up. The psyche of a fertility-troubled woman with multiple miscarriages simply astounded me.

The test came up negative, as I knew it would. I returned to the pre-op area where Kevin was waiting for me. Dr. Haney came in a short while later and for the first time, I met the man who would operate on me that day.

He was tall and lean with a bald head. The little amount of hair he had was nearly white and cut very short around the sides. The thing I noticed most was he had some of the kindest eyes I'd ever seen. They had a twinkle to them and perfect little creases that made it obvious he laughed a lot in his life.

He shook my hand affectionately and made a point to talk to Kevin. He explained to us again how the TAC would work and what exactly he'd be doing in surgery. I was a nervous wreck, as I always was before surgeries. The truth is, the majority of my surgical history involved D&C's, and those did not leave warm and fuzzy memories.

Dr. Haney took my mind off my nerves by going on and on about how one of my brown eyes was lighter than the other. I had known that all my life of course, because when I was a baby, one was blue and one was brown, but in my toddler years the blue one shifted to a different shade of brown. Only two people had ever noticed and yet this renowned doctor with a lifetime of experiences wouldn't stop going on and on about it. He showed all the nurses and anesthesiologists in the operating room. My last memory before the anesthesia sent me into a deep sleep was a swarm of surgical-masked faces peering down at me to get a look at the amazing eyes Dr. Haney couldn't shut up about.

Before I knew it, I was waking up from surgery feeling groggy and out of it, yet hopeful. The procedure was such a drastic thing to do to my body just to try to have a baby. I knew it was an act of desperation and there were no guarantees, but I couldn't shake the newfound HOPE that maybe this was everything we needed all along.

We were to spend one night in the hospital and one to two nights in a hotel before Dr. Haney would clear me to fly. They brought in a horrible looking cot for Kevin to sleep on, but I knew he'd crash on it with no problem. The man could fall asleep anywhere. For the first twelve hours after surgery, I slept. Mostly thanks to the pain pump safety-pinned to the front of my hospital gown. The morphine was amazing and kept me in this delirious state of dopey.

The nurse came in sometime later and told me that I needed to get up and walk. I'd gained a lot of inside tips on recovering from a TAC surgery from my online *Abbyloopers* discussion forum, dedicated strictly to women with TACs. They called themselves *Abbysisters*. I had found another incredible online network of women and hope.

Through my research and feedback from the *Abbylooper* women, I had learned that walking after an abdominal surgery is enormously beneficial to recovery.

So I pressed a U-shaped travel pillow against my incision for support and feebly made my way through the halls of the huge hospital.

Kevin and I took a cab to the north side of Chicago after we were discharged. We found a hotel room with an in-suite kitchen and living room to make my recovery a bit easier for us. Kevin ran to a Target nearby and gathered some groceries to get us through the next two days.

I diligently walked the courtyard and hallways with a pillow pressed against my incision. As I passed a woman who looked to be in her forty's with short brown hair, she looked at me knowingly and asked if I'd just had a C-section. How was I to respond to this question without getting way too personal? *Oh no, it wasn't a C-section. I actually had a transabdominal cerclage placed because I keep miscarrying babies and this is supposed to help.* Um, awkward.

I just nodded back at her and she proceeded to blab on and on about how she had a C-section too and walking was so good for it, so I should keep up the good work. I inwardly prayed she didn't ask to see this new baby of mine. Never mind why the heck I would be in a hotel after just having a baby.

After getting a wheelchair escort through O'Hare International Airport, we finally made it home and I couldn't wait to start trying to conceive. Dr. Haney informed us that we could begin our attempts as soon as we wanted to. He made a joke the day after my surgery when I asked when we could start trying. He said if we were that eager, he only asked that we prop a chair up against the door so we didn't give his nurses heart-attacks!

It was two weeks before I felt well enough to do the deed. After three months of negative pregnancy tests, we went back to our RE and used the same protocol that got us pregnant three times before. Again, it worked on the first try. The due date for our new little nugget was May twenty-fifth, the exact same date I had my TAC placed one year prior. If that wasn't a sign from up above, I didn't know what was.

Dr. Patel suggested we continue doctoring in Chicago for the pregnancy so she could closely monitor everything. Despite not being super impressed with her care thus far, I was too scared to disagree with anything she requested of me. All I knew was that I wanted no regrets. If I refused to go to Chicago for pregnancy monitoring and eventually miscarried, I would have always wondered if things would have turned out better had I listened to the doctor.

I visited Chicago four times in my first trimester for an ultrasound and consult with Dr. Patel. We got cheap flight prices through Southwest Airlines out of Omaha, Nebraska. It was a two and a half hour drive from Sioux Falls, but the time and money saved was well worth the inconvenience. We managed to fly in and out of Chicago all in one day, so we only had to take one day off from work. We got off work, drove down to Omaha in the dark, stayed at my college friend, Maureen's house and quietly left her place at 5:00 AM to catch our 6:30 flight. We took a cab to the hospital to arrive in time for our 9:00 AM appointment and then took a bus back to the airport as soon as we were done. There was no time for sight-seeing. We saw the airport and the hospital and that was it.

Kevin was able to come with me three out of four times. The one time he didn't come was because of the cost. I told him it really wasn't necessary for us to buy two plane tickets for one measly appointment and it would be best for me to go alone to save money. I knew the real reason Kevin didn't want to miss an appointment was because he never knew when we would have *that* appointment—the appointment where they told us everything was over and that another baby had died on our watch.

With a lot of convincing, Kevin finally agreed and let me go by myself. Dr. Patel was my official doctor for my first trimester in Chicago and ordered all the ultrasounds and had consults with me every time we visited. However, Dr. Haney continued to pop his head in on all my ultrasounds. He was just cool like that. I never received an additional bill for his extra visits and he continued to remain at my beck and call throughout the entire pregnancy. He replied to a number of scary emails that I sent complaining of aches and pains. Eventually, I realized the ultrasounds in Chicago were the same as the ultrasounds in Sioux Falls and the Chicago doctors weren't giving me anything I couldn't get in Sioux Falls. So once I got through the first trimester and things seemed to be staying calm in my uterus, I felt comfortable enough to discontinue doctoring in Chicago and had my maternal fetal medicine specialist and hematologist in Sioux Falls manage all care from then on.

***

14: IS IT TIME?

Paige, Amy's Postpartum RN

As a postpartum nurse, I was able to be part of a very important time in a patient's life, the early days of transitioning into a family. The call from the Charge nurse came early in the day that I was going to get a C-section patient. I sat down to look up the information I needed to care for the patient. I found the name, age, and medical history pertinent to my care. I also looked to see how many children the patient may have at home. That is when I realized it was going to be a special day. I was going to be part of the care for a woman that was not a first time mother, but would be taking her first child home. As my breath caught in my throat, I said a small prayer for the family, five lost babies and finally a baby to take home. Having had a few miscarriages myself, I could only imagine how overjoyed they would be. I was nervous for them. A newborn at just thirty-six weeks could easily end up in the Neonatal Intensive Care Unit. While no parent wants this to happen – I did not want it for this particular family – they had already been on such a long journey.

Friday was my turnover day. The day I went from thirty-five weeks pregnant to thirty-six. It had been a normal day at work, nothing too crazy. When I arrived home, my cramps felt pretty persistent. Typically, I ignored my cramps because they had been so consistent throughout this pregnancy.

I looked over to Kevin with my eyebrows scrunched together, "I think I should be counting these cramps. They are sort of coming in waves of intensity, like contractions. I should probably see how many I have in an hour, don't you think?"

Kevin raised his eyebrows, "I suppose you could, but you know what the doctor said—it's just stretching and making room."

After laying on the couch for a little over an hour, I realized that I had counted six painful waves of cramps. "I think I'm going to call the on-call number."

This was a first for me. So far in the pregnancy, we had never had to go to the emergency room. This was a miracle in and of itself. But it was definitely not something I would talk about, for fear of upsetting the God above, and being stricken down for counting my proverbial chickens before they hatched.

However, in the first trimester of the pregnancy, I had experienced some light bleeding that continued well into the second trimester. There was a reason for this. Our little thirty-six-week baby that I was now pregnant with—had a twin.

***

They missed Baby B at our first ultrasound in Sioux Falls when I was only six weeks pregnant. So for about a week I was under the impression that I was pregnant with just one baby. After the initial ultrasound was when we began doctoring in Chicago because Dr. Patel wanted to keep close tabs on me.

At seven weeks pregnant, Dr. Haney was actually the one to inform me there were two babies inside me. He popped his head in during my ultrasound to see how I was doing and to inquire about my cervical length. He glanced quickly at the screen and said, "Oh wow! Two!"

I looked over at Kevin and then back at the doctor. "What do you mean, two?"

Dr. Haney looked smug. "Didn't the technician tell you yet? Yes, there are *definitely* two babies there!"

"Two heartbeats?" I croaked. How could I possibly have missed that? I was a self-proclaimed expert on ultrasounds and I didn't see anything back in Sioux Falls! What was he talking about?

"Yes, although, this one's heart rate is pretty high, tachy even. It also looks to be measuring about a week smaller than Baby A. It's possible it could be a vanishing twin."

I'd heard that term before. It was so mythical sounding. When one twin dies earlier in the pregnancy, the mother carries it until it naturally breaks down and *vanishes* in the womb.

For a whole week, I let my imagination run wild about the prospect of twins. I remember excitedly texting my best friend, Ashley, that I had flown in to Chicago with one baby and was flying home with two. I knew when I texted her that I was getting way ahead of myself. Even though I had a long history of miscarriage, and Baby B measured small with a tachy heart rate, I couldn't stop myself from fantasizing once again about having two adorable little babies in my life after all the hardships we had endured. It was just too hard not to be excited. *I was pregnant with twins!*

When I went back for another ultrasound a week later, sure enough, Baby B didn't have a heart beat anymore. I was besieged with grief on the loss of a fifth child. *Five. How utterly obnoxious.* I had barely known I was pregnant with twins, but the loss of Baby B reminded me of how this may have all been for nothing. Big. Fat. Nothing.

I went home after my ultrasound that day, stripped down to my underwear and bra and crawled into bed. Kevin crawled in behind me and spooned me as I cried a familiar cry, relived a familiar heartache, and recalled well-known memories that still shook me to my core.

The next day I called my friend Kristen, who worked at the hospital I miscarried at, and asked her if she could get me another gold ring for my necklace. I felt nervous and incomplete not having all five of my babies represented around my neck. The drama of this loss was pretty minor compared to my other losses but this baby still meant just as much.

The doctor had warned me that vanishing twin syndrome could cause some spotting and cramping, but by the time I delivered the other baby there would likely be no evidence of the loss. Thankfully it was very sporadic and light. About halfway through the second trimester, I had stopped bleeding all together. The small amounts of spotting I had endured were a cakewalk compared to my history of bloody episodes in prior pregnancies! It had been months since I'd had any real cause for concern.

***

Even though I was at thirty-six weeks with no major episode, I was still uneasy as I waited to be transferred to the on-call midwife. I always hated speaking to anyone that wasn't my doctor because I was such a complicated case. It was no fun to ramble off that I had a large history of recurrent pregnancy loss past the twelve-week mark, a blood clotting disorder or that I was on high doses of blood thinners and had a transabdominal cerclage, which meant I required a C-section. It was a big fat list that screamed, *complicated*! I felt like if they didn't know me they would brush off my symptoms as though they were nothing to worry about.

The midwife told me to go to the store and get milk of mag because she thought I was constipated. Kevin marched off to the store like the devoted husband he was, and after I found some results from the chalky drink, I thought I felt some mild relief.

However, the next morning I still had severe contractions. I called the midwife again and she told me to take more milk of mag. When I used the restroom a short while later, I wiped out some red blood—VERY different for this pregnancy. I was reasonably concerned. I called and got the same midwife. She sounded annoyed and told me to *just come in.*

When we got settled into the triage area of Labor and Delivery, I put on my hospital gown and belt that monitored contractions around my big belly, and the nurse confirmed I was in fact having regular contractions. Thankfully, my doctor was on call and came in to see me shortly thereafter.

He entered the small curtained area and sat on the stool at the foot of the bed. "Well, you are having contractions and since you are thirty-six weeks and one day now, I think it's best to just go ahead and do the C-section now, especially with that cerclage in there.

I sucked in a big gulp of air and felt pressure rising in my chest. "You want to deliver today?"

He nodded his head thoughtfully and scrunched his lips to one side, "I think it would be best as I don't know what laboring on that cerclage could do. I think it's better to be safe than sorry."

My emotions surprised me as tears and fear overcame me. "I'm not ready," I exclaimed, "I thought you'd send me home. I thought this would be nothing. I was really shooting for that thirty-seven weeks and five days mark. May ninth! I finally believed we'd make it to that point."

He looked at me with a small smile, "You've been begging me for weeks to take the baby. I thought you'd be happy with this news."

I wasn't though. I couldn't be. I was scared shitless. I didn't know what I'd expected but it wasn't that! Despite the fact I was having what I believed to be contractions at thirty-six weeks, I was surprised he wanted to deliver. I prided myself on being quite knowledgeable in the medical profession when it came to pregnancy and infertility, and yet I didn't see it coming. *Jeez, Amy. Get ahold of yourself!*

I looked over at Kevin to see if he was freaking out as much as I was. He seemed surprisingly calm. When it came to doctors and medical situations, he always followed instructions like the good little child he probably always was.

After I reminded my Maternal Fetal Medicine specialist that I had taken a blood thinner shot the previous night, he realized we couldn't do the C-section that day because I wanted to be awake during the delivery. Since I was on a blood thinner, I couldn't have a spinal anesthesia within twenty-four hours of my last dose. So, if we proceeded with the C-section that day, they would have had to use traditional anesthesia, which meant I'd be asleep during the whole birth and I did not want that.

My doctor agreed to try a shot of terbutaline to calm my contractions and see if that would slow things down until the following morning, giving the Lovenox a chance to get out of my system. The nurse wasted no time giving me a shot in the arm and the meds had an instant effect of taking my already rapid nerves to a near tipping point. I felt anxiety, pressure and nervousness tingling throughout my body while the drugs worked their magic. My doctor told me they would keep me overnight and they would schedule the C-section for 9:00 AM the next morning, if everything stayed calm. I was not allowed any food or drink all day in case things became more urgent and they had to deliver before then.

A tall, thin nurse came into the triage room with a wheelchair a short while later. "Hi there, we have your room all ready for you. Are you ready to go?" she asked perkily.

I adjusted the belt that was monitoring my

contractions and brought my feet off the bed. "Yep, we're ready," I said trying to close the back of my gown so my butt wouldn't hang out.

The nurse came over and unhooked the contraction monitor cord from my belt and helped me settle into the wheelchair. She pushed me out the door with Kevin following closely behind carrying my purse and clothes. As she turned down a few different hallways, she was approaching a door to a room that looked very familiar. I felt anxiety build as she pushed me through the doorway to the room. Kevin looked at me nervously.

I let out a horrible sounding sob, "I'm sorry, I can't. This won't work. This room is bad!" I started bawling uncontrollably and struggled to get up out of the wheelchair.

Kevin put a steadying hand on my shoulder looked at the nurse apologetically. "Sorry ma'am, but are there any other rooms open?" He looked around uncomfortably. "We lost our last baby in this room."

I looked into the bathroom to be sure I had the right room. I did. I most certainly did. I pictured my bloodied self, holding our dead baby over the toilet in my bare hands. I struggled to hold back the cries that had escaped from my mouth. I was embarrassed for making such a big deal of this, but I couldn't help it. *I had to get pushed into this room, of all rooms.*

The nurse looked horrified and flustered, "Oh my gosh. Yes, I'm so sorry. We can get you a different room right away."

She settled me back into the wheelchair and pushed us out the door. I took one final look back at the room that had beaten us once before. I hoped no more horrors awaited us.

Once we were settled in our new, nightmare-free room I prepared myself to call my mom and tell her the baby was coming early. Kevin was texting away on the big couch along the wall that unfolded into a little bed. As soon as she answered, I started bawling. "Mom, they're delivering the baby tomorrow," I said, sobbing. I couldn't help it. The news was finally setting in.

"What Amy? What's going on? What happened?" my mom exclaimed trying to figure out the details between my snotty sobs.

I wiped my nose with the back of my hand. "Last night, I was feeling funny cramps and the midwife thought it was poop related, but this morning I was bleeding and now they are telling me they're contractions and they need to get the baby out."

"Amy, it's okay, just calm down. This isn't good for you. I'm sure you're going to be fine. You are at thirty-six weeks now, right?"

"Yes, but I really wanted to make it to thirty-seven, I

thought we would make it to our May ninth date Mom. It's still April for God's sake."

"I'm sure your doctor is making the right decision, Amy. If the baby is ready to come out then you just need to prepare yourself."

"What if she can't breathe? Or what if she has to go to the NICU? Or what if she doesn't make it?" I cried, rubbing my forehead.

"Amy, calm down now. You need to just relax and keep your body calm so you don't escalate things. You have a good doctor and you are in a good hospital. Just focus on those positives and try to relax. Dad and I will get in the car and be there this afternoon."

I ended the call and Kevin came over and rubbed my back. "You have got to calm down, babe. It's going to be okay. Remember, this is what you've wanted all along, to get the baby out. They are going to keep a close eye on you tonight and tomorrow. Everything will be just fine."

The day went by relatively quickly thanks to the various visitors we had. The doctor had me on IV fluids so I didn't dehydrate and irritate my uterus. I suffered from cottonmouth because they wouldn't allow me to eat or drink anything all day. My friend Ashley visited and helped pass the time. Mostly we talked about the events that led up to going into the hospital and everything the doctors told us.

My old OB/GYN came by to see me. I hadn't seen her since our very first pregnancy, because after that, I was considered high risk and only saw high-risk maternal fetal medicine specialists. "Hey Guys," she said in her unforgettable scratchy voice. "I saw your name on the patient admittance list and just had to come say hello."

I smiled thoughtfully at her. "Oh, thanks, doc. Yeah, the early labor is a little unexpected but they tell us things should be okay," I said nervously.

"Are you kidding? Things are going to be great!" she exclaimed as she stood at the foot of my bed in her white lab coat and pointy-toed heels. "You're at a great gestation. The baby is going to be fine."

"I keep trying to tell her that, but she's just so nervous," Kevin said.

"That's completely understandable. You guys have been through a lot. I keep tabs on you and try to check in to see where you're at. Man, you guys deserve this baby so much. You've been through hell and back," she said as she crossed her arms over her chest.

I nodded, agreeing with her sentiments exactly. "Do you know what we should expect with a baby born at only thirty-six weeks gestation?" I anxiously asked her.

"Most babies' lungs are pretty good at thirty-six weeks, but there is a chance the baby could need a little help breathing. Either way, it's going to be minimal help and not a huge issue. Really guys, this is a great gestation. Try to relax, okay?" she said as she rubbed my leg encouragingly.

We chatted for a brief time more and then my sisters came to say hello, so the doctor said she'd come back and visit in our postpartum room after the baby was born. I said a silent prayer in that moment that we'd really get to that point. Since my sisters had arrived to keep me company, Kevin went home, packed my hospital bag, grabbed our laptop and got some food.

Kevin's mom happened to be in town that weekend doing some rummaging, so she was happy she got to be there for the big moment as well.

Around 7:00 that evening, the nurse said that since my contractions had stayed calm, I could have something to eat. I ordered a grilled chicken sandwich and the baby's heart rate quickly shot up to the upper 180's while I was eating. I called the nurse to ask if the baby was okay and she smiled and said the baby must have been excited to eat.

Earlier, the nurse asked if we wanted to see an on-call chaplain or pastor. We decided seeing a pastor to say a prayer for us was exactly what we wanted. The pastor gave us a book of prayers and three rubbing stones that we were to hold when we prayed. We got three stones that said *Hope, Strength* and *Peace.*

After the Pastor left, the nurse came in and offered me a sleeping pill to help me get some rest that night. I saw every hour on the clock. *Apparently, sleeping pills would not work on a woman with recurrent pregnancy loss praying for her first live birth.* Finally around 5:00 AM I admitted defeat and got up and showered. After drying my hair, I crawled back into bed and hooked the belt back around my belly that monitored the baby's heart rate. Once I was satisfied with the heart rate, I leisurely put on makeup since I knew we'd be taking pictures today.

The neonatologist came in around 7:00 AM. He was a short, older man with glasses and light brown hair swept back to the side. "Hi guys, I hear we're going to have a baby a little early today."

My eyebrows pulled together, "Yes, should I be nervous?"

"Well, I'd say about half of them need a little breathing assistance. Their lungs aren't quite fully developed. We'll assess the baby in the operating room and make our decision. If the baby does need help, we'll have to take her to the neonatal intensive care unit for a bit. Your husband is welcome to come along, but you will still be getting stitched up at that point. Some babies don't need any help at all. But if she's less than five pounds, she will automatically have to go to the NICU."

Kevin and I looked at each other and smiled. "Well, about three weeks ago, the ultrasound said she was already seven pounds, so I don't think we have to worry about that," Kevin said as he squeezed my hand reassuringly.

The doctor smiled, "Okay then, I'll see you in there."

A few more medical professionals came in to prep me for surgery. I had butterflies fluttering all over and I was still a nervous wreck. The nurse that started that morning was really sweet, Micaela. She was pregnant too, pretty far along by the looks of her.

"When are you due?" I asked her anxiously, to get my mind off my nerves.

She grinned widely at me. "May thirteenth. Only two weeks from now."

"Holy cow. You're still working here. Jeez, sit down for a little bit, Kevin can help me with some of this! I exclaimed as I walked slowly from the bathroom dragging my IV cart along beside me.

She laughed sweetly and said, "Oh, I'm just fine, you're the one that needs to take it easy. And you'll need to take that necklace off before we go too, so don't forget," she said as she was typing into the computer next to the bed.

My hands instantly went to touch my five gold rings hanging from an old leather strap around my neck. My five gold rings for my five angel babies. I swallowed and silently prayed I would not make another angel.

I fumbled the clasp behind my neck and suddenly, the clasp broke and all five gold rings fell to the cold linoleum floor, clinking along the bed rail on their way down. "Kevin. My rings, they fell! Oh my God!" Shock and panic washed over me. *It's a sign. A bad sign. My baby isn't going to make it! My angels are telling me to prepare for the other shoe to drop. Another nightmare headed our way.*

I sat on the side of the bed while Kevin and Micaela searched the floor to find all five. Tears threatened my lower eyelids and I whispered, "This is really bad. This can't be good. I'm losing her Kevin." My chin trembled and my face twisted in pain as the tears poured down my face and sobs fled from my throat.

Micaela looked up at me seriously, "No, this isn't a bad sign. This could be a *good* sign! Your angels are telling you it's time to let them go and move on! You're having this baby Amy."

Her using my name in that moment made me believe her more. It gave her credibility, like she knew me and therefore knew what was going to happen. I worked hard in that moment to pull myself together. I sniffed and took a deep breath. It was time to go.

Micaela settled me back into the wheelchair that would take me to the operating room. "Kevin's not going to be able to come in until they get the spinal placed, but they'll bring him in as soon as possible. I'll be with you the whole time. Okay?" Micaela said looking between Kevin and me reassuringly.

"Okay," we said in unison. Kevin reached over and grabbed both my hands that had been balled up above my belly. "I'll see you in there, okay?"

"Okay," I croaked out. I had lost it. I was a wreck. There was no use pretending I had it together.

"Relax, babe. Everything is going to be fine. I'll see you soon." He kissed me hard on the lips and opened his eyes. Before he pulled away, he looked at me deeply, in search of the reassurance he needed to let my hand go. I looked into his eyes and saw all the pain and anguish in them that I'd seen so many times before. We were broken, together. Ruined forever.

Amy Daws

15: LORELEI HOPE

Micaela, Labor & Delivery Nurse

Five losses. My heart sank as the overnight nurse gave me the patient report before I assumed my role as Amy and Kevin's nurse for the day. Five losses in a row? How horrible. How did they make it through that? I had known the pain of losing a baby myself, but could not imagine five times in a row. I was certain they would be nervous and scared among many other emotions. But that day would be so different from the pain they'd endured in the past. That day would be a joyous day. As a labor and delivery nurse, witnessing births was a daily occurrence for me, and was always a miracle. But that day would be an extra special miracle. I would help Amy and Kevin experience the birth of their baby, the baby they had waited so long for. I prayed the Lord would let it go smoothly. I asked him to watch over us as we worked, and guide our hands and decisions. I asked him to fill me with words of wisdom and encouragement and to please bring their baby into the world safely, and give Amy and Kevin the overflowing joy of the miracle they deserved. It was an honor to have been a part of it.

I gingerly walked into the operating room. I looked around and saw masked faces busying themselves all around me. It was amazing how surgery on one person required so many hands on deck. I was fighting back tears as I approached the operating table. The anesthesiologist sat me down on the side of the bed and explained what he would to do to my spine. I was scared of everything at that point, so it was no surprise to me when I sobbed yet again.

Nurse Micaela, who was masked and cloaked in her blue surgical scrubs, came over and held my hand. I bent at the waist and did my best to hunch over my thirty-six-weeks-pregnant belly, to afford the doctor better access to my spine. Micaela stroked my shoulder while they worked and the tears flowed down my face onto the cold, hard floor.

In that moment, all I could think of was the baby and if she was alive. *What if her heart stopped? What if the cord was wrapped around her neck? What if she couldn't breathe? Would they check to make sure she was still alive before they cut me open? What if I bled too much and they had to do a hysterectomy?*

The needle hurt going in, a lot. The anesthesiologist fed me encouraging words, but all I could think of was that I was in pain, and how terrified I was of how it would end.

A couple of nurses and the anesthesiologist quickly laid me onto my bare back and bottom at that point. I quickly felt a warmness creep over my right side, "I feel more warmness on my right side, is that normal?" I asked, unsure what else to say.

They quickly tipped me onto my left side. I assumed that the meds needed to disperse more onto my left side. All the modern medicine advancements in the world and they used gravity to help dispense meds.

After a short time I felt warm all over and they laid me flat on my back. They lifted up the bottom of my hospital gown and tucked it up on top of my chest. As they set up a curtain just below my chin, I looked up at Micaela and asked where Kevin was. Just then he came walking in wearing blue scrubs with a matching scrub cap and mask. All I could see were his blue eyes looking at me as he took in all the equipment around me.

"You gotta talk to me babe, I'm freaking out right now, talk to me about something," I said as I felt the lower half of my body begin to disappear.

Kevin looked at me sideways like he was torn between looking at me or what they were doing to my belly. He realized he needed to focus on helping me relax. He reached up and rubbed away some of the tear residue. "They are just getting started," he said excitedly. "Hey, guess who else is here right now?" he said.

"Who?" I asked nervously.

"Nurse Amy. Remember her? She was the one that was with us during our twin loss," Kevin said, his eyes wide.

"Seriously?" I questioned.

"Yeah, she came and got me to bring me back here after I got my scrubs on. She's pregnant too! She asked me if I remembered her and I felt bad because I didn't. She offered to take pictures for me too. How cool is it that she's here today of all days?" Kevin stated incredulously.

It was amazing. I had a brief moment of fear that it could be another bad sign, but the anesthesiologist interrupted my wandering thoughts and asked me if I could feel any sensation when he touched me below my chest. I felt nothing, so the medical team began their work.

While I lay there, all I thought of was all of the times I'd been here before. All the times I walked into that hospital pregnant with a baby and walked out empty handed and brokenhearted. When I closed my eyes I saw the horrific scenes that had taken place in my bathroom, bed, office, and hospital. There were multiple locations of nightmares at my disposal. This was my fourth pregnancy and I had lost five babies. I didn't think it was possible it would turn out any different.

The doctor intruded my thoughts, "Okay Amy, we're going to pull her out now, you're going to feel a lot of pressure. Just hang in there."

Suddenly it felt like a five-hundred pound man was

sitting on my chest and somebody was standing above that man pushing down on him. The pressure in my chest was so intense. I didn't know how I was able to breathe. "Oh, this feels so weird!" I cried.

"They are pulling her out now, babe." Kevin's voice was rising alarmingly high at the end of that sentence. "Oh my God. She's out! It's her! Holy cow!"

I looked at Kevin, slightly startled, because I'd never heard his voice sound like that before. His eyes were huge and the little bit of skin that showed around his surgical mask was beet red. "Do you want to cut the cord?" our doctor asked.

"No, I better not. I'm shaking like crazy and I don't want to screw anything up," Kevin said, laughing slightly.

A second later I looked up to see what Kevin was seeing and then I saw her. My creation. My daughter. Her mouth was wide open as she let out a gargled little fussing sound. She had big pink, juicy lips and dark hair, wet and slicked down against her head. The doctor brought her over to my face for just a few seconds, then took her over to the exam area where they would assess her health and breathing.

Kevin looked at me wide-eyed as my chin trembled and concern washed over me, "Go over there, Kevin. See what's going on and if she's okay."

Kevin walked over to the area without another word. I looked over to where they examined her, just ten feet from me but I couldn't see much of her because the nurses and doctor surrounded her.

"Is she okay?" my voice cracked as I uttered the statement that could make or break my heart.

And then she cried a cracked, raspy sort of cry. She sounded like me with a deep, raspy voice like I have had my entire life. She was my daughter!

The medical staff all laughed out loud as we listened to her dramatic pleas to get her warm and cozy before she really flipped out.

"Do you want to know what she weighs?" the doctor looked over and asked.

"Yes," I uttered. *Duh dude? Why wouldn't I want to know!*

"Six pounds, eleven ounces," He said and the staff all let out approving replies, heads nodding.

"Oh my gosh. She's a little peanut. We thought she was going to be huge," I said as I laid there waiting while they finished their assessment.

The doctor came over and said, "She's breathing well and I'm pleased with her test scores, so we'll let you keep her here and hold her while they finish stitching you up. She can go straight to post-partum with you. She won't need to go to the NICU."

My heart swelled at the pride I felt in that moment. My baby passed her first test with the odds against her. *And I got to keep her.*

Nurse Micaela began swaddling our baby up nice and tight. She looked between me and Kevin and spoke loudly over our baby's continued cries, "You have a waiting room full of people, do you want me to tell them anything?" she asked expectantly.

"Yes!" I blurted. "Tell them that she's healthy and what her weight is," I said looking over at Kevin for reassurance. He nodded back at me excitedly.

"Are you sure *you* don't want to tell them what she weighs?" she asked walking over towards Kevin with the baby.

"No, I want them to know, they've been waiting for a while now, tell them everything about her!" I exclaimed excitedly looking at Lorelei in her hands and smiling at all the amazing people waiting to hear everything. Both my sisters were in the waiting room along with my parents, Kevin's Mom, his sister Megan and his brother Tony, his wife and their two kids. They were all here for us. I never imagined I'd have a whole waiting room full of people. I thought that was something you only saw in the movies, but our family had all been on this journey with us from the beginning. They may not have always said or done the right things in the right moments, but how could they? I was in hell for five long years. There was nothing anybody could say to make things better—or stop me from being jealous, angry or upset. My feelings weren't rational but they were necessary for my survival. Yet our family supported us, through and through. Their hearts hurt when ours did and their emotions would swell just like ours as they learned of our miracle baby's birth. *Finally.*

"You want to take her over to meet her mommy, Dad?" Nurse Micaela said as she eagerly looked at Kevin.

Kevin awkwardly shook his head. "I don't trust myself to walk over there holding her, so I'll sit down by Amy and you can hand her to me, okay?"

"Whatever you want, Dad," She said smiling.

I was still lying on the table with the curtain at my chest, so there really was nowhere for me to hold her. Kevin sat next to me on his stool and carefully held our daughter. She was wrapped tightly up to her chin in a white thermal blanket with a pink and blue cloth hat on.

I reached out to touch her. "Hi baby. Hi! I'm your Momma. I'm your—" I cleared my throat quickly as my eyes brimmed with tears. "—Mom."

Instantly she settled down like she was soothed just by the sound of my voice. In that moment, my heart and my mouth spewed out everything it had been dying to say for so long. I didn't care who heard all the deeply personal things that I'd been holding onto for so many years. I needed to let it all out to her. She deserved it. All of the things I would never allow myself to *assume*, or hope for.

For months I tried not to love her too much in my belly because I was scared it would hurt more when I lost her. I rejected my feelings for her because I was in a constant state of survival mode and I needed to protect myself. Now was the time for me to make amends for not believing in her. For not fully loving her as I should have. Even though I was lying half naked on an operating table with doctors and nurses buzzing all around me, I didn't care. *This was my moment and nobody was going to take that away from me.*

I told her all of the things I was scared to let God know I had been wishing for. I told her I loved her and that Daddy and I had been waiting a long, long time to meet her. I told her how scared we'd been those last few years, not knowing if we would ever get to take her home to live with us.

Her eyes softened as they adjusted to the new light and she blinked twice slowly as if she acknowledged everything I said. Kevin brought her closer to my face so I could kiss her round, soft cheeks. He held her there while I wept softly, a huge smile on my face.

In that moment, I felt a light turn on inside of me.

"It was always supposed to be you, wasn't it, baby? You were the one meant for us. You were what we'd been waiting on and hurting for all these years. Specifically you. Our baby, Lorelei."

I looked up at Kevin with happy anguish streaked all over my face. "She's the one, isn't she babe? She's the one that was supposed to be here."

He leaned down and kissed me over the top of Lorelei's head. He pulled away quickly as she screeched out another raspy cry. I laughed through my tears and soothed her with my voice again, "It's okay bunny. We're just so happy that we got you. You were worth everything. *Everything.* You have a lot of angel brothers and sisters in heaven that are going to look out for you your whole life. They were just making room for you. You were supposed to be our miracle."

I smiled and kissed her and continued to cry happy tears. I didn't believe that this could happen for us. I didn't believe we would become parents. I spent months and months of my life trying not to get attached to those babies. I tried so hard to harden myself so I wouldn't break apart and die when things ended badly, as they always had before.

The truth was, my babies had me from the start. They were in my heart before they were conceived. And losing them killed me inside, but there was a greater plan for us. We needed to look at the big picture. The big picture was Lorelei; *specifically her*. She was who we were always supposed to have. Why did I have to lose five babies to get to her? Maybe someday I would know. I *hoped* someday when I got to heaven, I'd meet those five angel babies of mine and they'd sit me down and explain it all to me. We'd all laugh at how silly grieving for them was. I *hoped* that was true. I *hoped* that someday I would see the whole big picture and it would all finally make sense. But in that moment, we didn't get to know. If we had known, what would faith be for?

Lorelei Hope Daws was our miracle baby—our everything! She brought the light back into our lives. There had been so many dark days. And those would never fully go away for us. We'd always have a small pain in the deep dark corners of our eyes. We'd always have a catalog of nightmares in our heads. Despite the fact that we finally got her, we still lost five babies. How does one ever get over something like that?

Lorelei Hope fixed us. She didn't take away our past, but looking back now; we would never want her to. The perspective those angels gave us was profound. They were part of us and always would be. They shaped who we have become. We are better friends, better listeners, better parents and better people because of them. Those angels of ours ruined us and saved us, all because we never gave up *hope*. Maybe we have more than one miracle after all.

***

Amy Daws

EPILOGUE:

It took weeks and weeks of calling and recalling our family members to set the date. But finally the big day was upon us, Lorelei's baptism. Lorelei was nearly six months old and the most adorable butterball of a baby we'd ever seen. When she was born at six pounds, eleven ounces, she was all skin and bones. By the time we were discharged from the hospital, she only weighed six pounds. I was concerned with the amount of weight she had lost, but the doctor assured us it was normal and she'd gain it all back in a couple of weeks.

Still, I couldn't get past the fact that the first thing most people said when they saw her was how skinny she was. I was developing a complex because of it! She wouldn't breastfeed well and after a couple of weeks when her weight dipped to just below six pounds, I finally gave up on breastfeeding and decided to strictly pump and bottle feed her.

Once I decided to stop the arduous process of breast-feeding, Lorelei's weight took off. She developed a huge round tummy that fit just perfectly in the palm of my hand and the pudgiest, mushiest cheeks you could ever imagine. Her dark brown hair had lightened and thinned some, providing more of a peach-fuzzed baby head that felt amazing on my lips.

Our house was full of family in town for Lorelei's baptism. Sunday morning, we ran around like crazy getting all of the items ready to take over to the church early. We'd planned to have her baptized at the 10:45 AM church service, and serve a meal afterwards in the church fellowship hall. My Mom and Grandma made hot turkey sandwiches, pasta salad and Jell-O squares. Kevin's Mom decorated a big sheet cake with a cross on it that said *God Bless Lorelei Hope.*

We had to hurry out the door because we had a lot of setting up to do and the pastor wanted to meet with us and Lorelei's Godparents to discuss the details of the service. We selected my sister Amber and Kevin's brother Tony to be Lorelei's Godparents. Selecting Godparents was a difficult task, because it meant we had to leave someone out. Kevin and I agreed that family would be the most appropriate choice for Godparents. Our older siblings were established in their own families, so we agreed they were a good fit. It was important to us to have representation from both Kevin's family and mine.

We arrived at the church quite early to set up and our parents, our grandmothers, our siblings and their families were there to help. They decorated long banquet tables in the fellowship hall with vintage children's Bible storybooks that my mom brought from their church. In between each book were little baby footprints on pink and blue paper that said *Walk With God*.

I carried Lorelei in her infant car seat carrier through the church halls and into the large kitchen attached to the fellowship hall. My mom was busy setting out dishes on the buffet counter. "Hey Amy, we've got all the food ready to go and I have Lorelei's baptismal gown hanging over here," my mom said coming over to greet me.

"Great," I said, hauling Lorelei up on the counter. "We should probably get her changed because the service will be starting soon."

The gown Lorelei wore was the same gown worn by my mother and myself when we were baptized. It had an empire bodice with a cream chiffon overlay that hung down past her feet. The dress had embroidered crosses and designs in a vertical pattern and tiny cap sleeves with a lacey scalloped trim. It fit Lorelei perfectly. I found a shabby chic cream flower on a thin elastic band to wear on her head.

My younger sister Abby came over to help get Lorelei's outfit changed. "Hey, I have a gift for Lorelei that you should open now because it kind of goes with her outfit," she said as she helped me maneuver Lorelei's onesie over her head.

She handed me a small black velvet jewelry box. Inside was a tiny baby pearl bracelet with a silver cross and charm. The charm was engraved: *Lorelei Hope.*

"This is beautiful Abby! Where did you get this?" I asked her. I was excited how perfectly it went with her baptismal gown.

"I found it from a seller on Etsy actually," she said as she clasped it around Lorelei's chubby wrist.

"Well, it matches perfectly, thank you," I said smiling warmly at her.

Kevin came over and looked over Lorelei's outfit approvingly. "Wow, she looks so cute!" he said as he helped me shove her old clothes back into the diaper bag. "We better go sit down, my family is saving seats."

We stowed our belongings in the kitchen and headed toward the sanctuary. Our family was so large we occupied the first two rows. Thankfully Lorelei took a catnap during the first half of the church service. I was nervous with how she would behave because she had a tendency to be a fussy baby. She preferred to be bounced and walked around a lot; so sitting down during the service was a bit nerve-racking. Just before the pastor called us up to the altar, she woke up.

I beamed through the proceedings. The pastor addressed Kevin and me first—then the Godparents, and finally the congregation. I held her over the bowl of holy water as our pastor cupped and poured the water onto her head. Lorelei behaved perfectly. She was simply stunning with her cherubic, fresh-faced, bright and innocent eyes.

After the pastor dabbed Lorelei's head dry, she took her from me and wrapped her in a prayer blanket they made, and walked around the altar to introduce her to the congregation.

After the service, we took some family pictures outside of the church on a pretty bench with lattice fencing and large green bushes directly behind it. Lorelei captured everyone's attention as she smiled for pictures. Everyone was busy chatting and enjoying the beautiful sunny, September day.

We had one final thing we wanted to complete before we went in to serve lunch and eat. Prior to church, I asked my dad to go pick up five white balloons. I wanted Lorelei's baptism to be a day to acknowledge our angels and to say a formal goodbye in front of our family. I didn't want Lorelei to grow up with a constant reminder of her angel siblings being brought up at every special event in her life. She deserved to have a normal life free from grief. However, I thought her baptismal day was an appropriate day to honor them.

My dad handed me the five white balloons, each tied neatly with a white ribbon. I handed Lorelei over to Kevin and grasped the bundle in my hand while my dad cut the weight that was attached to them off with a pocketknife. His expression was a little sad and uncomfortable.

My pastor's voice cut through the chatter. "Can everyone gather around for a moment," she paused as she made her way over to Kevin, Lorelei and me. "We're going to say a prayer before we head inside to eat, but Amy and Kevin have some words they would like to share first."

I looked over at her with a strained smile on my face, and then out to my family as they waited for what I was about to say. I reached over with my free hand and grabbed Lorelei's chubby fingers and gave them a gentle squeeze for courage. "First of all, thank you all for coming today. I'm going to make this quick because I don't know if I could get through it all otherwise."

"Kevin and I are so, so thankful for our sweet baby, Lorelei. We waited a long time to become parents and she is the best gift God has ever given us. But we never want to forget the babies we have lost…" I paused as my voice cracked. I looked around nervously at everyone's faces and zeroed in on Kevin's younger brother Adam who was visibly choked up. *Well that sure as heck doesn't help.*

"Everything we did was for them. Lorelei has five amazing angels to look out for her the rest of her life. These balloons are for our five angel babies. We love you and we miss you always," I said crying freely at this point. I looked over at Kevin for reassurance and released the five white balloons up into the sky.

A moment of silence came over my family as we watched the balloons travel up into the sky, all five stayed close to each other, even though they weren't attached. After another couple of minutes when we could barely see the balloons anymore, I cleared my throat and nodded to our pastor to let her know it was okay to say the prayer for our meal.

We made our way inside and assembled in line for the food. A couple of minutes later, my seven-year-old nephew, Evan, came rushing up to me from outside. "Amy. Amy!" he exclaimed slightly out of breath from running.

"Um, um, we were watching the balloons in the sky you know…and um, they came back," he said, his big chocolate eyes turning wide in amazement. "They flew away and then they all came back, all together," he said as if trying to explain it better.

"That's awesome buddy," I said affectionately squeezing his shoulders into my hip.

Kevin came up to me with bright eyes, "Yeah, we were out there watching them and all five balloons circled all the way back toward the church and then sort of floated away again. Cool right? All five still together."

I furrowed my brow. "Really cool. How does that happen?" I asked amazed at the meaning behind this.

"I don't know, but it's pretty neat," Kevin said as he nodded his head incredulously.

It wasn't neat. It was *incredible*. It was as if our five babies were communicating something powerful to us. It was like they were saying, *hey Mom and Dad, even though we're not there with you, we'll never be far away and we'll always be with you.*

And they would. They would always be with us and always hold a special place in our hearts. It was through their lives that we learned how to never stop *Chasing Hope* and how we got our very own, *Lorelei Hope*.

***

*Stay tuned for Book Number Two of Amy's story: Chasing Peace
The tale of Nevaeh and finding peace in her journey.*

.

.

Amy Daws

ACKNOWLEDGMENTS:

When I think about whom to thank for this book, I first have to thank God for the strength He gave me to write it. It was hard at times, but I'm so glad I was able to do it.

I also have to thank all my friends and family who read this prior to publishing. You guys gave me the inspiration, encouragement and motivation to continue writing when it all seemed like way too much to handle.

My sister Amber Blume, thank you for all your insightful feedback in the early days of this project and for squeezing me into your busy life. My bestie, Ashley Caskey. I can always count on you for honest and sarcastic advice! When you told me it was good enough to keep going, I knew I had a chance. Kathy DeLuca, you are my online bestie! I still have the initial text of you gushing over my story saved in my phone. You were my first reader and number one cheerleader girl! My childhood bestie, Desiree, thank you for taking me seriously on this journey and for using your blog to champion it along the way. My legal brain, Maureen Cosgrove. Your comments were so incredibly helpful. The nurses at Sanford, you guys are all amazing and special and so so important to me. Paige Rock specifically, I will never ever forget your beautiful words. I so needed to hear them. Sarah J. Pepper, a legit author who gave me my first real dose of the reality and craziness of self-publishing! You are amazing! And everyone who contributed testimonials that gave my book an incredible personal touch.

Huge thanks to my editor, Heather Banta. I never knew what working with an editor would be like and you made it exciting girl! You didn't treat me with kitten gloves and I'm so glad for that because I know that my book is the best it can be because of that!

Elizabeth Petrucelli. You came in to my life by accident and I can't imagine what this process would have been like without you.

Thank you to my parents for always being there for me and never letting me feel like I was alone on this journey. I'm thirty-something years old and not ashamed to admit I still need my mommy and daddy!

To my hubs, Kevin. We made a family babe! I don't think I would have made it through all those hardships without you by my side. Your unending optimism was the perfect contrast to my negative pessimism. The yin to my yang. The cheese to my macaroni. You loved me through it all and most of all; you kept hope alive for us when I was ready to crumble.

To my Lorelei, my sweet miracle from God. Jeez girl! I can't believe I get to keep you! To think that I could have called it quits so many times and never have made you is unimaginable. Your sheer presence kissed a bad owie on Mommy away, my love. You made Daddy and me all better. We are drawn to the love and light that gleams from your soul. I fully believe the spirits of your angel siblings shine in your eyes sweetie. They are so expressive and that was no accident. They tell a story. They tell a story of a Mommy and a Daddy whose hearts hurt so much from a lifetime's worth of disappointment, they didn't think they could ever be happy again. You proved us wrong. As soon as I met you, I knew. It was always supposed to be you. Your eyes shine with hopeful thoughts, dreams come true, and prayers answered. I wrote this so you would always know how hard we fought for you, how much we wanted you and how perfect you are for us. It was always supposed to be you.

To my angels in heaven. My sweet precious angel babies. This book is entirely for you. Everything we did was for you. Someday I know I will meet you all and I cannot wait to thank you for the tremendous gift you gave me in my life. Though I only held you in my body for a short time, I will hold you all in my heart and soul forever. Mommy loves you.

FOR MORE ABOUT THE AUTHOR

www.amydawsauthor.com

www.facebook.com/chasinghopebyamydaws

Twitter @amydawsauthor